The History of Atherstone Research Team is a Local Heritage Initiative, funded by the Heritage Lottery Fund and Nationwide, through the Countryside Agency. The project has been managed by Atherstone Civic Society.

H.A.R.T. also received funding from The Market Towns Programme, an initiative designed to help to bring new life to rural towns and improve them for the good of the people that live and work in or around them.

Once upon a time in Atherstone

Margaret Hughes

with

The History of Atherstone Research Team

Illustrated by Amanda Gould

Published by the Atherstone Civic Society

Grendon Lodge

Long Street

Atherstone

CV9 1BA

Printer: BIG in INK Ltd

0800 085 1518

First Published 2005

ISBN Number: 0-9551803-0-9

This is the first book from the History of Atherstone Research Team; a second will follow.

H.A.R.T. has chosen to present some of its findings first of all in an informal, 'easy-reading' format – and what more 'easy-read' is there than a story? However, the second volume will offer a collection of expert papers covering a much wider range of research, and presented appropriately as a work of academic depth.

Acknowledgements

Members of the regular HART team:

Marion Alexander, Dave Atkin, John Austin, Eileen Barrs, Mary Bates, Jim Beechey, Andy Benson, Roger Brayford, John Charles-Jones, Brenda Collins, John Connell, Gary Crump, Lorna Dirveiks, Betty Dutton, Isabel Edgar, Chris File, Dave File, Chris Green, Grace Green, Pauline Gurney, David Harding, Loraine Harding, Joan Hogg, Margaret Hughes, Joyce Jackson, Phyllis Johnson, June Maidens, Maureen Mercer, Mary Morrison, Mary Mortimer, Sue Naylor, Celia Parton, Val Pickard, Rita Poulson, John Steed, Rosemary Steed, Fred Sutton, Mike Trye, Howard Vero, Judy Vero.

HART would also like to thank all members of the committees, together with the local people who kindly allowed the survey team access to their buildings, or lent their deeds; also Lynda Barber who helped with administration.

Thanks are also due to HART's professional advisers:
Dr. Nat Alcock, Sue Brown, Alan F Cook, Judith Drever, Bob and Jean Meeson, Jonathan Parkhouse, Dr Terry Slater, Janet Spavold, Dr Andrew Watkins.

CONTENTS

INTRODUCTION

My father had a term that he used in a peculiarly dismissive manner whenever authors' flights of fancy struck him as particularly far-fetched: *figments.*

His term has returned to me as I seek to explain what has happened in the creation of this book, because this is a book that may be regarded as a collection of 'figments'.

Lucius the Roman surveyor is a product of my imagination – there is no historical record of a Lucius – he is a figment. Hubert the scrivener, and Betty alongside her bailiff – all three plod Atherstone earth as figments. Dick Simcott whirling across the town, Tilly patiently waiting her moment – nowhere in the records will you find evidence that they existed – figments, both.

Thomas Hear is in a different category. Thomas existed, the records show it, but his search for his treasured wife Theodosia – that is a figment, just as is the behaviour that I have allowed to Theodosia, and to her Daniel – figments. The connection of any Pennsylvanian literacy movement to Atherstone's real life Ann Hood and her real life stepmother Sophia is yet another figment.

So, please note the statement at the head of each chapter that spells out in utter clarity what is fiction and, by implication, what is fact. Take it in conjunction with each chapter's Notes to produce for you a 'health warning', loud and clear: "Don't believe everything you read".

But then, my father hadn't heard of 'faction'. My figments are seriously and indivisibly bound to fact. Lucius's Manduessedum is carefully constructed from recorded evidence. Hubert the scrivener must attend to the multitude of known, if somewhat dry, facts put into the mouth of the historical figure of William of Harden. Betty and her bailiff inhabit an Atherstone circumscribed by recorded detail. Dick Simcott, and Tilly and her mother Anne Partridge resonate against a thicket of known, incontrovertibly documented fact. The plethora of recorded fact that underpins Thomas Hear's day is exceedingly rich, as is the vibrantly documented background to Little Jo's existence and his fascination with his Pennsylvanian find. Look in the Notes to each chapter, and you will find the sources that anchor my figments to fact.

The actual number of fictional characters in the book is relatively small – fourteen altogether, and of these only five are major players: Lucius, Hubert, Betty, Dick and Tilly. On the other hand, the stories are crowded with real people, real in the sense that some record of them, however slight (it may be only a name) does exist. But you need to be aware, once again, that around these I have spun a web of fiction. Lifestyles and appearances have been supposed. Emotions have been imagined. Personalities and moralities have been imposed (in a few cases not always flatteringly; apologies may be due to anyone recognising an ancestor in my imaginary portrayals).

But my intention is to honour. I offer these stories as a memorial and a tribute to the forebears of today's Atherstonians, (mindful of 'forbears' in the sense of 'fore-be-ers' – those who used to be). As a result of working on this book I find myself unable to walk through Atherstone without meeting in my mind's eye the shifting impressions of those who, over the centuries, shaped the town and were shaped by it. In my mind's eye buildings rise and disappear and are replaced, the town's topography forming and reforming like a film made by time-lapse photography. I think of Shelley's "light footfalls of spirits passing through the streets."[1] Today's Atherstonians live out of, and alongside, their predecessors.

An anecdote that comes from another town (Cirencester, but let's take it as 'anywhere') powerfully depicts this sense of the past coexisting with the present. "In the 60s he saw a whole ghostly congregation when he was attending a service in the Parish Church. They were dressed in very old-fashioned clothes and seemed to be following a different order of service, as they stood and knelt at different times to the real congregation. He didn't find them frightening, no-one else was aware of them, and they were not aware of the real congregation."

---

[1] Shelley: Ode to Naples

I'd like to think that when next you walk down Long Street, or cut through a passage from there to the Bus Station, when you stand in the Market Place or visit the Leisure Complex, you may think of the swish of a passing skirt, the scent of a long clay pipe, the myriad sounds of two millennia of life.

> *A fair field full of folk found I there,*
> *Of all manner of men, the mean and the rich,*
> *Working and wandering, as the world asketh.*
> Langland:The Vision of Piers Plowman c1370

Margaret Hughes   October 2005

How to read this book

- You may find it helpful to read the Notes *before* the chapters.
- At the beginning of each chapter, note the fictional characters.
- The timeline that precedes each chapter sets local events in a wider perspective.
- Where appropriate, the chapter Notes give a chronology of fictional events.
- A map accompanies the later chapters to help you not only to follow the events of the chapter but also to relate the Atherstone of that time to the Atherstone of today.
- You may find it interesting to plot the cross-chapter links of some characters. A brief reference or a 'walk-on' part in one chapter sometimes has more significance in another chapter. You will also be able to track certain properties and sites.
- The graph at the end of the Notes visualises the growth of the town's population, the impact of which on the town's day-to-day life being an underlying theme to these stories.

- Or, of course, you may choose to read the seven stories simply as stories to be enjoyed for their own sake.

What dictated the choice of year for each chapter?

The narrative potential afforded by particular events in the historical sources governed the choice of year in which each story is set.

Key sources.

Will and Inventories

A wealth of information was derived from wills and inventories held at the Lichfield Record Office, and wills in The National Archive. A great many of these have been transcribed over the last thirty years by Atherstone Local History Group, led by Marion Alexander.

Atherstone's Manor Court Rolls

Atherstone is unusual - and fortunate - in having retained records of copyhold transactions in the Manor Court Rolls from the 14th century to the 19th century. Each time a property changed hands the Manor Court Roll recorded the transaction: from whom, to whom. What's more, the owners and/or occupiers of the adjoining properties are also named. Very often occupations are given, sometimes with family connections and incidental detail. Sometimes wills are recited. This information has been the exciting core of this project of the History of Atherstone Research Team (H.A.R.T.). It is enabling the production of a large number of Atherstone 'house histories'. And it is my source - and inspiration - for much of the story-telling of the later part of this book - Chapters 5-7.

(You will find an explanation of the copyhold system in Dom Edmund's words in Chapter 3, pages 50-51, and in the Notes to Chapter 3, page 55)

The 1786 map of Atherstone

The 1786 map has been central to the researches of the H.A.R.T. It shows as still discernible the boundaries of those ancient burgages (for an explanation of which see the Notes to Chapter 2, page 41) allocated by the Abbot of Bec in the 13th century. It gives all the properties along Long Street and around the Market Place, and names each owner. It allocates a number to each property, and indicates whether it is freehold or copyhold. Now using these numbers, it is possible to provide the locations of many of the properties in this chapter.

There are 2 copies of the map at Warwick County Record Office (WCRO), one being WCRO P26, the other - deposited by Howard Vero's family - catalogued as CR2511/21. This latter is a later copy, on linen, bearing the name Charles Vero. Several other copies exist, one being with Atherstone Town Council.

CHAPTER 1

NATIONAL EVENTS	AD		LOCAL EVENTS
Roman invasion of Britain	43		
		50	Establishment of Military Fort at Manduessedum (Mancetter)
Seutonius Paulinus Governor of Britain	58		
Boudica's final battle	60		
Rule of Emperor Nero		65	Establishment of Manduessedum burgus (villa and farmsteads)
	68		
		75	**Lucius returns to Manduessedum**
Gnaeus Iulius Agricola Governor of Britain	77		
Destruction of Pompeii	79		
	100		

CHAPTER 1

LUCIUS RETURNS

A.D.75

Lucius and his host are fictional characters

The grizzled face of the old Roman relaxed as the contours of the earthwork defences of Manduessedum[2] came into view a couple of miles ahead along the Watling Street. The road before him out to the west seemed to be running directly into the late afternoon sun.

Lucius squinted into its strong rays to verify that this was indeed the site he had recommended all those years ago as the best place for Watling Street to cross the River Anker. He allowed himself a sense of satisfaction as he recalled the role to which he had been assigned, a mere year or so after arriving in this island as part of the invading army, sent by Emperor Claudius, Aulus Plautius at its head.

---

[2] The Roman name for Mancetter

He was proud of the astonishing swiftness with which his counterparts had put in place a military track linking Londinium with the mountainous strongholds of the Ordovices in the west[3]. He remembered how they had found it useful to study the route taken by the native mineral road already in existence, noting how it avoided high land and followed river valleys - a design philosophy adopted likewise in many places by his colleagues.

But he was even more proud that the young surveyor that he then was had been given the task of finding the most strategic and workable sites for the foundation of forts along its way. Now some thirty years on, a lifetime of service given to construction works all over this isle of Britannia, he was revisiting some of his earlier successes to see for himself how things had been further developed. He would visit Letocetum[4] next, in a day or too.

But time now to relax at Manduessedum, take a bath, have a good meal, sleep in comfort and shed his travel tiredness; tomorrow he would enjoy seeing the prosperity of 'his' settlement.

It was well placed, virtually in the centre of Britannia. Some few miles back from his present position he had crossed that other great Roman artery, the Fosse, that heads northward towards Lindum Colonia[5], and southward takes the traveller to the Severn estuary and beyond. As his horse brought him close to the settlement of Manduessedum, he looked around him along the level of the Anker valley. His glance took in the high ground off to the south west on his left. Those road engineers pioneering the line of Watling Street had had to face the fact that at the point where they actually must cross the Anker they could not avoid its flood plain. But continuing west from the river-crossing they had been able to chart a course that occupied a thin corridor of safe land, between the soft alluvial flood lands of the Anker on their right and the hard rocky soils of the hilly ridge that was on their left.

---

[3] i.e. in Wales

[4] Wall

[5] Lincoln

Very wooded, that rocky ridge: he remembered how it featured in his calculations all those years back. A good thing to have so much wood near to hand, outside any settlement - 'out woods', to offer much-needed fuel and building material. Protection, too; he had felt immediately that this small-scale landscape of low rounded hills, steep scarps and small, incised valleys gave a strong sense of enclosure.

Yes, he recalled, (his gaze running along the level line of the hilltop parallel to the road) also important to his project were the riches offered by these very rocks themselves. He remembered his excitement when, after several days of reconnaissance up there in the woods he had stubbed his foot against what he recognised straightaway as a once-molten rock obtruding from a drift of shaly stones. It looked rather like black granite, although quite soon he heard it called 'lapis viridis' by the stonemasons he brought in to quarry and work with it. And very useful the green-tinged stone proved to be, he reflected, in various local works both then and at the present time. Maybe even in times to come......

He had always had the sense that the works he initiated, along with that of his road-making compatriots and the settlers who inevitably followed, were somewhat trail blazing in this area. He reflected briefly on what may have been nothing more than a legend - although he was willing to give it the benefit of the doubt - the legend of people who populated the Anker valley before history began, men who used crude and scanty quartzite tools and lived in utter simplicity.

And yes, there were also signs of other peoples who had lived many, many centuries after them. One of his soldiers had kicked up a flint knife on a path by the river. And then, up on the highest point of the hills above Manduessedum there were the earthen remains of a fort of an older, earlier age, and a substantial mound fairly close by, that in his opinion was clearly a burial or memorial of some kind. And he had heard once that one of the farm workers ploughing close to Manduessedum's fort had unearthed a stone axe that may have been very, very old - so it had been claimed. But, given his expert knowledge of what is needed to support effective settlement, this elderly Roman surveyor had always believed that local soils and rocks for miles around were not suited to early peoples' needs.

Yet of course when he had first arrived there were the homeland Celts, living in their circular wooden houses with high sloping roofs, often close to the roadways they had put in place to support their own

existing prosperous trading economy. He recalled seeing the smoke curling from the centre of quite a number of those thatches, beside the Anker's slow and meandering stream, when he had arrived to judge the best position for the military fort so essential then as back-up protection for the Foss, and as a garrison to serve the increasing importance of the infant Watling Street. In this central part of Britannia some native Britons had actually been willing – glad, even - to help his work in a number of very useful ways. They were skilful horsemen, he remembered, and – fingering the dolphin brooch at his neck - fine metalworkers.

He was close enough now to be able to look southwards across the flat river plain, up to the military fort on the hillside, from which vantage its patrols had a clear view of whoever was moving along the Watling Street below. He noted once again the well-planned layout of the cluster of buildings that comprised 'his' fort, a large timber building dominating the group. It looks good and tight and well organised, he thought. Fit for the XIVth Legion who first held it.

He could see the roof of the temple, too, and found himself wondering whether people still made their votive offerings as they crossed the river. Surely still needed, he mused, in this present time. Constant vigilance must continue everywhere in the aftermath of that earlier terrible uprising, when Governor Suetonius and the army he led had come so perilously close to ceding victory to a native warrior queen.

These reflections brought him in sight of the ditches that were the outer defence of his objective for that day, the burgus[6] of Manduessedum. Nearby, lit by the sloping rays of evening sunlight, he could see people passing to and fro about their business: the smooth running of the nicely-established villa that was to offer him a hospitable welcome that night.

It grew chilly. Drawing up the hood of his goat's wool cloak, he allowed his imagination to stray to thoughts of the dinner probably even now under preparation. Perhaps there would be mutton from the flock of sheep grazing on the land by the river. Or locally raised snails? Lucius chuckled to himself to recall the last time he'd had snails. His host then, a bluff soldierly man, had had the snails carefully fed on nothing but herbs - some on basil, some on thyme or other herbs, some on garlic - before their final fattening on milk (with plenty of salt to make sure they drank more). But one snail, one single snail, was fed on bitter rue. There had been much jocular speculation as to which unlucky guest would bite on this one! Roars of laughter when it turned out to be the host himself!

But would there be vegetables tonight? He recognised afresh his original assessment of this damp and low-lying plain as unsuitable for extensive arable use. However, there were some good spots in this mixed quality farmland, certain areas easier to dig and sow, certain

---

[6] a villa plus farmstead

well drained stretches of sandy, gravelly soil that did fine for the basic arable farming to which his people were used.

What's more, the Watling Street carried a flow of trade to make good any deficiency. Might there be fish this evening, or shellfish? However, he felt sure his dinner would be enriched as usual with the anchovy sauce so essential to his countrymen's cooking. Thus anticipating, riding past the ramparts of the burgus, beckoned on by the comforting smell of wood smoke and cooking, the retired surveyor gave himself up to self-congratulation on being the initiator of such a thriving little outpost of empire.

His confidence in the prosperity of the settlement received further injections of evidence over dinner that evening. In his day, the findings of manganese in the hilly ridge above their plain had remained just that, findings. But dinner was served on pottery that his host told him had been made locally, of local materials that included, yes, manganese glaze. That, his host explained, was the key to the vibrant colours that brought the pottery to life.

After dinner, he led his elderly visitor to a spot by his villa's perimeter wall. There was still enough light for him to point out the glow from a small kiln just below the walls of the fort. Indicating the potter's workshop beside it, he invited Lucius to inspect the gravelled track that had been constructed to make easy the transport of the potter's output. "I can see," his host said, with unexpected passion, "I can see that we have all the right circumstances here, once others come to see it too, to turn this one potter's shop into an industry, my friend, a veritable industry. We could drive a thriving trade; why, even to far distances north through all the lands of the Brigantes, and wider. Perhaps not yet, but it will be so, of that I am sure."

The traveller was unprepared for such an enthusiastic lecture from his host, but was impressed nevertheless, learning that these local mortaria (mixing bowls with grainy interior surfaces) were produced from just the right kind of sandy, silty soil dug up from the underlying weathered quartzite in the woods on the ridge above. The grit that gave the bowls their rough insides was a mixture of different rocks. The charcoal that fired the kilns was burned from the abundant woodland. And the burgus had coal, too - wonderful black burning rock to defy the chills of winter - from an outcrop a mile away.

The pair returned to the dining room, where their conversation was helped along by good wine imported from southern Spain; the guest appreciated the finely wrought beakers in which it was served. How pleasant this was, he thought, looking around at his surroundings: the painted patterns on the plastered walls; the niche holding a graceful vase of milky glass threaded through with gilded strands like veins; the elegantly functional orange-ware flagon from which his host poured yet more wine. The warmth of the room enfolded him, the floor giving up stored heat acquired from hot air flowing from the furnace room through an underlying network of cavities.

Sleep came easily that night. At first. Until he woke with a start. Sounds of clashing metal, braying trumpets and the alien sound of bone-made clappers, pounding horse-hooves, shouts of men, screams of men, cries of women and little children, thudding of heavy wood on wood, again yelling, the rush of many feet scrambling close-packed on a muddy track........

He sat bolt upright, readying for what might be. He listened...... And let out a great sigh, for it had all been in his head. How could it not be? For such little time had as yet elapsed since the great routing of that formidable warrior Boudica and her frighteningly near-successful fighting force. She must have felt invincible, scorching Camulodunum[7], razing Londinium, sweeping on to utterly destroy Verulamium[8]. The memory was still strong in those who had been foremost in the taking-over of this northerly province.

Himself one of those first invaders, he knew very well that it had been military need that caused the so-prompt rolling out of the Watling Street. He also knew that a military road doesn't choose who marches upon it, friend or foe - an openness that Boudica was able to exploit when she used it to lead her massive eighty-thousand strong fighting force north west in chase of her Roman enemy.

So she found her enemy, and engaged in what was to be her final battle. They fought at...they fought..... the old surveyor struggled to think where they had fought. He lay down again, sleep befogging his mind. He knew that the battlefield had been approached by a narrow defile, and behind his brother Romans there had been a wooded area, while to their front they had had little or no cover, and they were on a plain. Manduessedum, he mused, how well that description fits Manduessedum. Was it here that Boudica fought and failed? But he fell asleep before he could resolve precisely whether such was indeed the case.

---

[7] Colchester

[8] St Albans

NOTES TO CHAPTER 1

Alan F. Cook provided the geographical, geological and agricultural information for this chapter. It offers compelling reasons as to why Mancetter, and then Atherstone, were sited where we find them today. You will find that some later chapters recall his reference to the "thin corridor of safe land, between the soft alluvial flood lands of the Anker on [the early road engineers'] right and the hard rocky soils of the hilly ridge that was on their left," where 'right' refers to the north side of Watling Street, and 'left' to the south side.

David Crystal provides an interesting commentary on the naming of the Fosse Way, upon which I've based my choice to have Lucius think of it simply as the Fosse. 'Fosse' usually means shallow depression, ditch or trench (in fortifications or roads), and typical Roman road profiles have a drainage ditch each side. Crystal tells us that in early sources the Fosse Way was sometimes called Fosse Street, and sometimes simply Fosse (and Foss). Crystal notes the criterion that the Anglo-Saxons used in selecting the labels 'Street' or 'Way'. Roman creations were 'streets' – Ermine Street, Watling Street; while pre-Roman routes were 'ways' – the Ridgeway, for example, and Icknield Way, overbuilt by the Romans. He implies the unsuitability of Fosse *Way* for both Roman and Anglo-Saxon use, and believes the name dates only from the fifteenth century. (Crystal, *The Stories of English* , Allen Lane, 2004; page 66)

This chapter has the first reference to the woods outside the town; they are described simply as 'out woods'. In Chapter 2 the 'out woods' are again present, but now referred to as 'outwoods', the term moving towards its more recognisable label - Outwoods with a capital O - which I use from Chapter 3 onwards.

Alan F. Cook notes that 'greenstone' (Spessartite Lamprophyre) "was used extensively in Merevale's Cistercian Abbey built c. 1148.....and is visible today in setts near No.19 Market Street, and certain blocks in St. Mary's Church."

There is as yet no conclusive evidence of the precise dates at which the Roman fort and the later burgus were established at Mancetter. It is agreed, however, that there was a significant Roman presence on the site at the date at which this chapter is set. For instance, one of the finds from excavations led by Keith Scott in 1977 is a pot dated 'not later than 58AD'. You can explore the issue further by going to accounts of archaeological surveys in the transactions of the Birmingham and Warwickshire Archaeological Society, 1998 Vol. 102.

Alan F. Cook notes that Watling Street was in construction in this area by 47 A.D. and in regular use by 74 A.D., according to some sources

Roman pottery production in the area is not in any doubt. A leaflet, *Roman Mancetter,* produced by the Warwickshire Museum, tells us: "Pottery was produced on a large scale in this area. Over 70 kilns and several tons of pottery have been excavated between Mancetter and Hartshill."

However, it didn't get under way to an industrial extent until about the beginning of the second century. Kay Hartley led significant excavations in the 1970s. She comments: "One might make a case for the very beginnings [of the pottery industry] going back to AD95 but that may well be stretching it. It went on until sometime in the 4th century, but it lost its markets in the north probably sometime between AD320 and 350 and production for the local market could have petered out in the second half of the 4th century..... Having said all of this, I believe, from the mortaria and other pottery which Keith Scott found, that there was minimal pottery production in association with the fortress in the first century, but there are no kilns known. This has absolutely no link with the later industry, it is just what one expects at fortresses in the first century when there were problems with getting adequate pottery of the sort they wanted."

Kay's advice points up the fact that I have credited Lucius's host with remarkable prescience!

I am grateful to Jo Connell for directing me to *The Pottery Kilns of Roman Britain,* supplementary series 5 (Vivien G. Swan HMSO1984 ISBN 0 11 701203 3) which includes a reference (p.99) to "Excavations by Mrs. K. F. Hartley, 1973a and unpublished." Jo points out that the Hartshill/Mancetter industries are usually known as one and the same.

Kay Hartley's finds included a Roman glass furnace, a rare find in England, about which she advises: "The glass industry itself was not rare in Roman Britain. What was rare was actually locating a glass furnace and ours [the Manduessedum find] was so small that it is obvious why they are rarely found. In any case, that also is second century. The glass furnace is more or less published in the following book: *Glass,* Ruth Hurst Vose, London, 1980. p.132-134; "*Roman glass-furnace at Manduessedum"*, description, and plate 38."

Other finds from Keith Scott's 1977 excavations included some Samian ware, (although I have not provided Lucius and his host specifically with Samian ware), and a bronze dolphin brooch which I have pinned on Lucius's cloak.

A delightful encounter with the "Combrogi", a 'living history' re-enactment group at Chedworth Roman Villa in the Cotswolds, resulted in my inclusion of 'snail roulette' – the dining game that climaxed with one unfortunate diner lighting upon the single bitter-flavoured snail. This unappetizing practical joke was explained (and part demonstrated!) by Combrogi chef, Ken Wiltshire (August 14th 2005).

The "graceful vase of milky glass threaded through with gilded strands like veins" describes a vase found at Alcester, now in that town's Roman Museum. (You may wish to contemplate imaginary reasons for its imaginary journey from Mancetter to Alcester....)

Boudica, Boudicca, Boadicea? Just how should we spell the noble lady's name ? Peter Salway (*Roman Britain,* 1985, Oxford Clarendon Press) goes along with Webster (reference below), and this is the version I have adopted.

Debate continues as to the site of Boudica's last battle. Marion Alexander tells of "the vague description given by Tacitus, who said it was approached by a narrow defile, with a wooded area to the rear of the Roman army, who were upon a plain with little or no cover to the front". If you are interested in pursuing this intriguing hint, you may like to read G. Webster's *Boudica: the British Revolt against Rome A.D. 60* published by Batsford 1978, and Antonia Fraser's *The Warrior Queens*, (Phoenix, 1988). It was Antonia Fraser's description of the battle that prompted my reference to bone-made clappers.

CHAPTER 2

NATIONAL EVENTS			LOCAL EVENTS
	1000		
Battle of Hastings	1066	1066	Hugh Earl of Chester given the Manor of Atherstone
Domesday Book	1086	1086	Hugh gives Manor of Atherstone to the Monks of Bec
	1100		
		1148	Merevale Abbey founded
	1200		
Henry III	1216		
		1239	Abbot of Bec buys a market charter for Atherstone
		1246	William de Guineville's suit against the villeins of Atherstone
De Montforts defeated at Kenilworth	1265		
		1279	William of Harden begins 45 years of Bec stewardship
		1289	Abbot of Bec revises layout of town centre creating the Market Place
		1292	**Hubert visits Atherstone**
	1300		

CHAPTER 2

HUBERT THE SCRIVENER

1292

Hubert the scrivener[9] is the only fictional character in this chapter.

Where Romano-British potters had sweated, and Romano-British ploughmen trudged, where Romano-British tradesmen dealt and Roman order had prevailed, now, many hundreds of years on, the little township of Mancetter lay peaceably around its stone church, between hills and river.

In the countryside above and beyond the church on a clear Lenten day in 1292 two men were riding towards Atherstone.

The cold winds of March whipped at the travellers. William of Harden shrunk his gaunt frame deeper into the rich folds of his cloak as his younger companion, in plain white habit, gazed stalwartly ahead,

[9] someone whose job involved writing, or making copies of, documents and books.

around each bend hoping for a glimpse of the little market town that was their destination.

Setting his face to the north wind, so unusually cold that Spring, Hubert the scrivener thought of the many miles he and his superior, the chief steward to the Bailiwick of Ogbourne, had covered since they started out days ago from their Wiltshire cell. Their journey that day had led them through Coleshill's busy hillside market place. Then at Bentley they had taken an hour's sojourn in the chapel, welcoming its airy surrounds cleared free of the forest. Now further along the road, woods once again hung all around, and a mile or two of road remained to be traversed.

"Not yet, Hubert my friend" said William dourly to the young scrivener, "some way to go as yet."
"Well then," came Hubert's stolid response to the knight, "as I know so little of our task, let's use these miles to repair my ignorance"
"Your ignorance needs best clear - as should these lowering clouds - if you're to be the valuable scrivener our Prior needs. Well, we shall reach the town, and we shall have good lodgings, from which shelter I must watch, and check, and count and measure, and you must record, and send to the Prior a full account of the prospering of the Manor here. And we shall do this well, for we must be found faithful."

"But sir, beyond our Prior does there not stand one other, one greater, the lord Abbot in Normandy? For I have seen the Prior's careworn face bent over letters thence. And once I was chosen to scribe his reply to one of those letters. I wrote with my utmost care, for fear of error on such import. The Abbot had demanded that our next report, (he called it our next 'status domus'), should show greater returns from our Prior's administrations: *The great Abbot of the Abbey of Bec-Helouin in Evreux sends greetings to his cell in Wiltshire, the Priory of St George in Ogbourne, and begs leave to know of his Prior how much......* Oh, and how much this....and how much that!

"Right sadly then did the Prior bemoan Atherstone's lack of a Borough Charter. 'Had but our lord the King Edward granted a charter as indeed he hath to other towns' – he named Stratford as one – 'then would our good town of Atherstone have its tradings roundly boosted.' Atherstone's revenues go to enrich the Abbey in Normandy, I warrant?"

"You understand most readily, master scrivener." William permitted a frosty smile to cross his pinched features. As true for Atherstone as for the Abbey's twenty-three other manors scattered across this land. So has it been for long years, aye, from some two hundred years ago when King William first conquered, and took this Manor of Atherstone from its owner then. That was Edwin, and he was the son of the lady, Godiva, of whom the tale is told. King William wasted no time before giving it to his nephew. Perhaps you've heard his name? Hugh, first earl of Chester?

"Hrrrmph!" William glared morosely. "Givings away and passings on. Within but a few years Hugh shifted the Manor yet again, gave it away. I warrant he had what he craved of it: a place in heaven, by the beneficence of the Abbey of Bec. And indeed it brought no harm to our French Abbot. On the contrary: two hundred years of revenue. Not that it matters to me. A steward prospers when his master prospers. A steward makes sure all is running smoothly as it should."

His glance fell sharply on his companion. "And a scrivener shall keep good record of that, eh, Hubert?"

Hubert sidestepped the remark.
"Was it a rich Manor when King William took it from Edwin?" he deflected.

William snorted.
"Atherstone's never known riches! Many's the day when our Prior hath lowered his brows to see the rents from the place. Three years ago they were but a poor £8.0.3d. Little use to point out to him how far that exceeded his returns from other manors in his Bailiwick of Ogbourne....as paltry a sum as £3 from Monxton.
'Aye, sir steward,' counters he, 'and £22 from Ruislip, so praise no more your Atherstone!'

Yet could I have called to his mind that Atherstone is not a draggle-tail lagging behind all his other manors; no, no, fairly middling it is, fairly middling.

"But I will grant you, Hubert, receipts for wool *were* pretty low: £1.2s.3d. compared with those from the other estates, whose outputs ranged from 1s. 6d. to £19.18s.6d. For corn it was £3.13.1d. at Atherstone compared with the overall range of 11s. 8d. to £59.5s. On the other hand, forget not that Atherstone tenants bear no heavy burden in what they pay to the king in court dues and taxes - £7.5s.8d. See how low that lies in the whole range of what other towns pay: a range from 6s. 8d. to £55.14s.0d."

The steward was lost now in his own mental review. "...As regards area of land sown, for Atherstone it was 280 acres but this is difficult to compare with others. Crops sown were wheat, rye, the mixture of barley and oats that is called drage, barley on its own, oats, peas....."

Hubert coughed gently. William looked round.
"Eh? What? Mmmm, well, even when the great Domesday Survey was done, although Atherstone had the land for 5 ploughs, why, they only had men enough to work but four. Fewer than seventy people living there then - ".

" - and how did they live? Did they live in comfort, William my master?"
William shook his head in exasperation.

"Do you ever stay mindful of our theme, Hubert?"

He sighed, relenting.
"No doubt many of our Domesday folk lived in comfort well enough. I hear they built soundly, in good timber, well thatched with the straw of the fields."

The pair had started on the long decline towards the town.

"The Saxon folk before that, oh, five hundred years or more before King William, they had the good sense to settle next well-used crossroads and near (but not too near!) old Roman sites. So, good trading. The Atherstone to which we wend is at such a crossing. Look, this very road on which we ride will cross at the foot of the hill the ancient Watling Street - worthy well-worn road. Then, on goes our road northwards, taking travellers to Derby.

"And more, those settlers of time past saw there was land for their beasts and their crops, there beside the river Anker .... a thin corridor of safe land, between the soft flood lands of the Anker on their north and the hard rocky soils of the hilly ridge that was on their south – this hilly ridge on which our horses' hooves even now slip and slither, curses be on it"

Hubert knew better than to take up the steward's cursing. Although, like his master, he was uneasily aware that the dark close-pressing trees of this stretch of the road afforded sinister cover to ill-meaning rogues, ne'er-do-wells, outlaws.

He pursued his enquiries.
"For many....you said 'comfort enough for many'. What of the others?"

The steward was trained to precision, and was able to give a detailed reply. Not for nothing had he studied the relevant entries in the Domesday survey.

"As well you know, Hubert, the villeins[10] fared best. For a villein, then as now, is as good as a free man....except of course in relation to his lord, to whom he owes dues and services in exchange for tenancy of land. Eleven villeins had land enough, around their houses – aye, and farther afield also – to keep their households sufficiently nourished in all things. Another two were cottagers, less fortunate, though each did have a smallholding, a patch of ground with his house. But doubtless they had many a craft to ply, as well. And one poor churl, a bondsman, with nothing but the strength of his back to keep him and his own in this world.

"But that was then. From these folk and their children's children have derived two hundred years of rent for our Abbots of Bec, with more to come.....and more. Nowadays there are a few more tenants and - " (he held up a hand) "- before you plague me with the question I'll tell you: thirty-six in total.

And very light indeed are the villein services asked of Atherstone tenants – but little labour in the fields and little carrying and messaging. Not for Atherstone the responsibility of the arduous journey to Southampton with the cheeses so prized by our Norman friends. Atherstone tenants are particularly privileged. Leave such cheese-bearing tasks to the tenants of other Bec manors."

He gave vent to an uncharacteristic chuckle.
"Despite the strenuous efforts of our brother William de Guineville when he was Prior! I've read the account of his suit, years back. He wanted to wring more labour services from the villeins. He failed! Atherstone hath ever escaped light. Well, well, it frees good men to concentrate on craft and commerce, and that is the reason the Abbot so decrees it - but," (his features resumed their severity) "it fails to provide him with adequate labour for the size of the demesne.[11]"

---

10 tenant-farmers, owing onerous rents and services to the landlord.
11 the land within a medieval manor that the lord did not lease to tenants but reserved for his own use.

At this point the trees parted, offering a far-ranging prospect. The flat river plain showed green in the valley, stretching away northwards to wide expanses of higher ground, laced here and there through the trees with thin spirals of smoke that betrayed dwellings. A wagon was visible, moving steadily eastwards along the straight mark that was the Roman legacy of the Watling Street. Closer, between the forest and the road several log stacks awaited collection, evidence of recent fuel-gathering. They had reached the outwoods, the townsfolk's foraging territory.

Hubert felt a surge of pleasure. "The town, sir! Where is the town?"

"Soon enough the town, young master, if town it may be called," grumbled William. "Further yet adown the bends and steeps of this rough road - may God strengthen my weary bones yet awhile"

"But it *is* a town," insisted Hubert. " For did not the Abbot himself in far-off Normandy hear of the Watling Street - and did he not deem it a great high road, a way that must bear much vital traffic bringing people and goods from all over the land through this his fortunate Manor - and did he not understand it thus to be every bit as well situate as Coleshill, nay, even better – and did he not these many years back before I was born purchase from the king himself the right to hold a market, so boosting Abbey revenues with market tolls, fair tolls, stall rents, oh and court fines, and more new houses bringing him more rents, aye, and a pillory, and a gallows....." He paused as a shudder ran through him.

Then, recovering his enthusiasm, "...and did he not recognise other new street-towns appearing all over the land - and did he not therefore order the town to be laid out properly, for I remember two years ago all the plans and the talk and the eagerness and the winning over of the good townsfolk to re-align their plots and the trampling on those that were unwilling – and did he not direct there should be some new plots – and did he not –"

"Enough! Spare my tired ears! The March winds batter them, I need no more from you"

They rode in silence for a while.

The steward conceded. "All that you say is indeed the case."

He sat a little taller in the ornate saddle. "It was planned well." He nodded to himself as he recited the mathematics of it: "We used the strip pattern of the existing field plots beside this celebrated Watling Street. From them we made eighteen equal sized burgages laid out at right angles to the road; eighteen tenants thus received plots of land behind their houses. And further, we made for the town a market place. Indeed, our good Abbot chose to raise a fair stone chapel on its north side. The market place is large and rectangular, also at right angles to the road and abutting unobstructed straight onto that road. Busy, busy spot, buying and selling, producing sweet revenue for our Abbey. For that, seven tenants gave up, ahemmm - were persuaded to give up - their land by the Watling Street and around this market place, to make twelve brand-new burgages "

Then he shook his head in irritation.
"The folk going to and fro their plots of land with wagons and carts wear lanes along the backs parallel to the Street, each side, north and south! And then, between the southern back lane and the back boundaries of the burgage plots along the south side of the Watling they have established a triangle of land where they buy and sell their cattle.

"Well, you'll see soon enough ..... this very road from Coleshill comes into the town beside it......there's a pond on it. And you and me Hubert, we'll skirt this watering place, keeping the cattle market on our left as we plash through the cow-soiled mire," (Hubert hid his amusement at his senior's fastidiously down-turned mouth) "till shortly our road will meet the long main street, the Watling, where on the left-hand corner stands one goodly inn. A stout timber-framed dwelling, good thatch atop.....But we shall ride past, navigating the worn ruts of that long street before turning into the market place, where we shall find another, the Angel, at which inn, thanks be, they are enjoined to lodge and feed us, and find good oats for our horses."

He paused. "And Atherstone *is* good. It is a town, and it is good."

Hubert looked at his sober, irritable companion with a new respect. He recognised the man's deserved pride.
"Will it thrive, sir?"

The knight pondered. "Will it thrive?"

And on they both rode, willing it to thrive.

NOTES TO CHAPTER 2

Terry Slater provided information on the 13th century re-development of the town, and the layout of its burgages, streets and market place.

I have also drawn from Marjorie Morgan's book: *The English Lands of the Abbey of Bec,* published by Oxford University Press in 1946, but now out of print, and M.W. Beresford's papers: *The Origin of Mediaeval Boroughs in Warwickshire,* Warwickshire History Vol. 1 No.2 Autumn 1969, and *The Origin of Mediaeval Boroughs in Warwickshire: an additional note,* Warwickshire History Vol. 1 No.3 Spring 1970.

Alan Cook provided more information on landscape, and on the severe weather of the spring of 1292.

The bailiwick in question was an administrative area: the English estates owned by the Abbey of Bec in Normandy. It was run by the prior of Ogbourne in Wiltshire, and it comprised altogether twenty-four widely scattered manors, of which Atherstone was but one. The manor of Atherstone had been given to Bec by Hugh, Earl of Chester, nephew of William the Conqueror.

So the hierarchy in our story consists of a chief steward, William of Harden, answerable to the Prior of Ogbourne, who in turn answers to the Abbot of Bec. Young Hubert comes at the tail-end of that. In addition, there was local 'hands-on' administration: the manor of Atherstone would have had its resident steward, of local stock but appointed by the chief steward and accountable to him. Then the local steward would have appointed a reeve to assist *him,* who was supported by other officials such as a hayward and a woodward, watching over the meadows and the woodland.

I have allowed William of Harden to remain cautious in his estimate of the population of the manor of Atherstone at the time of the Domesday Survey. The Domesday record is of 5 ploughs and land comprising one virgate, (roughly 25-30 acres), 6 acres of meadow, together with woodland; with eleven villeins, two cottagers, and one bondman or serf. These specifics offer us various interpretations as to what total population is implied.

The Victoria History of the County of Warwick refers to the existence of a 12th century chapel of the Abbey of Bec, on the site of the chancel of today's St Mary's Church in Atherstone market place.

There are several possible routes that our pair of travellers could have taken. Given the various options, I have avoided assigning them any specific road. We may suppose them to have followed a route through the woods from Bentley, and suppose that when they "started on the long decline towards the town" they had reached what is to some extent today's B4116.

A burgage is a plot of land let by the lord of the manor to a tenant (the tenant holding it being known as a burgess). We are told by M.W. Beresford in *The Origins of Medieval Boroughs in Warwickshire* (see reference above) that a burgage was the 'lowest common denominator' of held land. Beresford continues: "The burgess [burgage holder] although not necessarily free of all manorial servitudes, nevertheless did hold the land on which he had his house by a tenure sufficiently free to enable him to pursue those specialist economic activities which marked him off from a villager [e.g. petty trading, simple handicrafts]." In a planned town like Atherstone they were laid out by the lord, often as here, in long parallel-sided strips running from the main street back to a lane behind it.

William's reference to "lanes along the backs parallel to the Street, each side, north and south" is a reference to today's Station Street and North Street. Station Street is popularly known as the 'back way' to this day.

The "triangle of land where they buy and sell their cattle" is the still discernible triangle of land between Coleshill Street and today's bus station, opposite the White Lion and behind the Red Lion. In earlier times there was a pond in that vicinity.

"Long Street" in Chapters 2 and 3 is just a long street, its users then calling it Watling Street, or simply the Watling. From Chapter 4 onwards it has become Long Street.

Our travellers have been promised oats for the horses. This is based on a footnote in Morgan (see reference above), page 21: "Monks of Bec and their servants in their journeyings across England were given hospitality in any of the manors that lay on their route....Manorial accounts frequently record expenses, for example at Cottisford in 1292 the oats account included two bushels for the horse of the prior, one bushel for the horse of the sub-prior." Such quantities presumably were meant to be used over a period of time.

CHAPTER 3

NATIONAL EVENTS			LOCAL EVENTS
	1300		
		1375	Augustinian friary founded on North side of Atherstone market place
Peasants' Revolt against Poll Tax	1381		
		1387	Abbot of Bec attempts to make all Atherstone bakers use his oven
	1400		
		1406	Abbey of Bec loses Manor of Atherstone
Tennis is banned	1420		
		1423	Tenants are ordered to share repairs of pavements outside their houses
		1458	Guild of Mancetter re-founded
Edward IV	1461		
		1477	**Betty & Dom Edmund return home**
Archery is compulsory and cricket is banned	1477		
Richard III	1483		
Henry VII first Tudor monarch	1485	1485	Battle of Bosworth
	1500		

CHAPTER 3

BETTY AND THE BAILIFF

1477

All characters in this chapter are fictional, apart from John Riggeley the Abbot of Merevale, Alice le Colier and Robert le Taylor.

For almost two hundred years the little town that the Abbot of Bec had redesigned astride the Watling Street had been going about its husbandry and its trading, its small-scale unshowy building of homes, its practical additions of simple market hall and friary chapel. It had continued its business unmoved by shifts in ownership. Indeed, some might say it seemed unaware of its passage from Norman abbey to English king, to duke, to earl, and, in 1462, to the Yorkshire Carthusian Priory of Mountgrace.

Moreover, it was almost equally unregarding of the widespread economic difficulties that had beset the land. Where many places struggled desperately to find labour for the agriculture on which they relied, Atherstone folk sturdily got on, fattening their cattle for market on fodder crops, developing a range of trades, drawing on the forests for timber and fuel, for nuts and fruit, wax and honey.

In this quietly thriving spot, busy with making and buying and selling, producing steady revenue for its lord whoever he might happen to be, two figures emerged into the failing autumn light of late afternoon.

"Come then, master. Come home, come."

Ushered by his servant from the inn where he had been presiding over the View of Frankpledge court, the bailiff stepped down onto the rough surface of Watling Street, the rutted surface of the timeworn thoroughfare made even muddier by heavy carts from the nearby marl pit. Betty's bustling frame seemed almost to envelop him as, kindly but brisk, she wrapped in her capable arms the rolls of documents that her master was charged with safekeeping.

Dom Edmund was glad enough of her attentions. He had overseen the twice-yearly View of Frankpledge courts for fifteen years now, since coming to the town when Mountgrace Priory took the lordship of the manor. Manorial responsibility was indeed heavy, and heavier still weighed the relentless pressure of the king's lawyers watching over the administration of the franchise. He sighed. Now that all the lands of the estate had passed to tenants, unlike in earlier times, what a complexity was added to the court's dealings!

And the constant demands of the other courts, the Little Courts, were wearing too. Almost every month saw him there, handling their stream of complaints: John, a common baker selling underweight loaves; William who was no true butcher selling ram's meat improperly slain; dung not fully cleared away from Butcher Row on the east side of the market; Nicholas the victualler who knew more of water than of ale; and so on, and on.... Bailiffdom was beginning to take its toll, despite the able services of his trusted reeve and a court held in a good inn where fair ale could be at his elbow to refresh the proceedings.

"Aye Betty, much ado again this day," he acknowledged wryly. "Hard pressed as I was to find the tithingmen, those ten good and loyal jurors I needs must have, yet still at cock-crow I feared we had but nine."

He shook his head in exasperation.
"Young Master Drayton, all unkempt, came sadly lackadozy late; how sorely did his father and brothers berate him. They themselves were all there betimes, and his uncle too. I left the young fellow in no doubt but that he must be in good time at the next, for then we shall have with us the chief steward himself, come from Mountgrace to inspect our ways. And his father in strongest terms bade him be mindful of the townsfolk's duty to bring forth known offenders, or themselves stand forfeit for the damage!"

Betty nodded wisely, for in the preceding weeks she had witnessed his concerned endeavours to find the requisite number of adult men qualified to be bound as security for the townspeople's good behaviour. What havoc a spate of illness could wreak in a little town!

"Well, home now, sir bailiff. There's juicy coney stewing over the fire."

She steered the bailiff onto the paving that ran alongside the string of cottages lining the Watling Street, fussing the while.

"Be mindful of the mire....I know today you've been ordering folks to fix their stones, so you may as well walk on 'em. Not for the first time folks have been ordered to fix 'em. My own grandfather - I remember when I was a child - he had to fix the stones before *his* door, and they're hardly any better this day! But deary me, I mind the lads will be looking at you under their brows for your orders today. As if it's not enough that the King himself should ban cricket, you come along and ban their bowls. *And* their ninepins! Even the children's penny-prick, shame on you. Why, some little ones have only just learned to tie the penny to the string, never mind learned how to hit it! And no more chess! What a sadness for the poor friars across the market place. For chess keeps their minds warm in their cold old friary....."

"Not so old, Betty. But one hundred years, that's all," interposed Dom Edmund in the interests of truth.

She flashed him a disparaging glance, and continued.
"Well that's as might be. I mind as long ago as the year of our Lord 1420 - so my father Hubert told me, he knew it for it was the very year he was born - *his* father was sorely grieved when tennis was forbade. Why all these frownings and forbiddings?"
"Because, my good Betty, flimsy pastimes promote idleness. So deems the Abbot of Mountgrace".

"Mmmm. Well. The Abbot lends *you* but little chance for idleness, master, charged with so much care to make sure no man carries a weapon. Would but your tithingmen had the watchfulness they are charged with on your behalf. There you must go, seeking out the intentions of strangers in our midst, watching all that they might be about. And stopping them from buying victuals in the market until our own good folk have bought their share. I hear you fined one of our townsfolk today for giving hospitality to such a wanderer......well, good riddance, say I.

"And naming no names, but you know and I know who's going to be sorely vexed at another of your rules from today –" Betty gave the words full emphasis – "No Loitering By Servants Around Houses At Night."

"Come, Betty. Nathaniel the miller's man is a good enough man"

"And I have enough work in caring for one man, who, look, cannot steer his course to keep out of the mire....."

Their gentle bickering occupied them as they picked their way down the long street and helped them ignore the warmth and sounds spilling from the many doorways marked out by ale-poles. They passed a toft, an overgrown plot where brambles covered walls that once were Roger the tailor's cot, abandoned to ruin by his widow sadly unable to find the rent. They passed Hall Lane leading away up beyond the cattle market towards the Outwoods, where householders cut their wood and foraged their pigs.

Betty juggled her bundle of rolls into a more secure grip. She derived a solid satisfaction from her task of caring for their administrator. Why, her grandfather Hubert, dandling her on his knee in the doorway of one of the long street's cottages, had told her he had heard talk that his grandfather – or was it his grandfather's grandfather? – even possessed the rare skill of writing, and once wrote some important letters to the very lord himself. She felt a vague sense of pride that her position somehow connected her to her ancestor's status of responsibility. There now, these parchments in her charge must be got safely into the wooden press in the corner of her master's chamber.

For Dom Edmund lived well. In the house of Hugh the baker he had a small hall with a warm and welcoming hearth, and his own chamber adjoining. The use of these comfortable quarters was his for life, for he had made a payment to secure it, a single substantial payment, making sure his two stables also were included.

Hugh's wife Alice, her daughters and Betty fared fine in sharing of the kitchen, even when the butter making was in progress, and Betty had found there a space to be cosy, close beside the bread oven that was almost always in use. (Dom Edmund had secured for Hugh the right to his own oven, which meant an end to tiresome daily excursions to the common bake house, albeit nearby; and, to Hugh's satisfaction, an end to paying the lord for the benefit of its use.)

Nowadays it is only as she falls asleep that she thinks of her poor Tom and sweet, tiny, new Elizabeth, both swiftly gone in the year the terrible sickness swept in (as it did so often) and took so many, aye, and Hubert her father too.

Tom - she remembers the proud flush on his face as he talked with her father - Tom had been so pleased to join Hubert as one of the brethren of the Guild of Mancetter, at the time it received a new lease of life. All the talk in the inns that year was of John Riggeley, good Abbot of Merevale, and his gaining of a new licence to re-found the Guild. She sometimes dwells a little on Tom's private hope that one Trinity Sunday, when the Guild elected its two masters for the year, one of those chosen might be him. Well, well. She has the comfort now of the Guild's priest saying mass for Guildsmen's souls, in Mancetter Church, right next to the Guild's hall.

And as she drifts warmly towards sleep, she puts aside her remembered storm of grief and fear, when kinless and homeless she sought how to live, until first Alice then the good bailiff found her skills and honest hard work necessary to their daily rounds. A home, a home again!

As for that that business of which Hugh the baker and Dom Edmund had talked so long and earnestly, with "surrendering this", and "admitting that", and "ingress" and "egress" and "easements", she was only too pleased to leave such matters to those who understood them. Dom Edmund had patiently explained to her that they were negotiating his share of the house before going together, Hugh and himself, to finalise the matter in the manor court. There Hugh would sell a share to Dom Edmund, and Dom Edmund would be recorded as the new owner.

It was all to do with the copyhold system. "The monarch," he had said with respect in his voice, "is the ultimate land holder. He gives lands to his lords and vassals in exchange, usually, for money and a fighting force. Likewise then these lords give lands to their tenants in exchange for services on the land and availability as part of a body of fighting men. But of course, dear Betty, here in Atherstone the lord's main interest has ever been for the good folk to ply their trades so that the town may thrive."

Betty had thought gratefully of her grandfather, her father, her honest Tom.

The bailiff continued. "Folk pay their copyhold fees to the lord and the lord asks neither for their labours on the land, nor for their blows in battle. And the details of these exchanges of property are all inscribed by me in these rolls that you now, good soul, tend so dutifully for your careworn master. Of course, the people take away their own copy of the manorial record....hence the name, my dear; hence 'copyhold'." He nodded thoughtfully. "The custom of tenure in Atherstone goes back to the Anglo Saxon period when kinship groups formed for security."

Betty liked her master's ways of speaking, although much of his meaning passed her by. But she knew that the lord of Atherstone manor was the Prior of Mount Grace. Dom Edmund often told her stories of his time in Yorkshire, in the years before he was sent to administer Atherstone's manorial affairs; to buy a share of a house; to give shelter to a homeless young woman.

They were nearly home now, darkness almost upon them. On the other side of the long street the market square opened out, edged by small shops of timber and thatch. Here Betty paused to get her breath. Glancing to the left up Hall Lane she saw that the dying sun was reddening the autumn colours of the Outwoods. Beyond the Outwoods but out of sight was the wooded pasture of Merevale Abbey. With some sadness she recalled her fruitless pilgrimage, (as over the long years made also by so many others), to the statue of the Virgin that stood in its gate chapel. She sighed a little: her puny devotion had been inadequate. Then, seeing that her master was well ahead of her, Betty lifted her skirt and picked her way as best she could across Watling Street.

Dom Edmund led the way onto the westward edge of the market place that people called Bakehouse Lane. Betty looked past him to where, over long years, a small chapel had stood; now the north side of the market place was bounded by the friary, with its little enclosure beyond.

Beyond that were glimpses of the wide Middle Field, where, harvest time now past, Hugh the baker's three cows grazed companionably

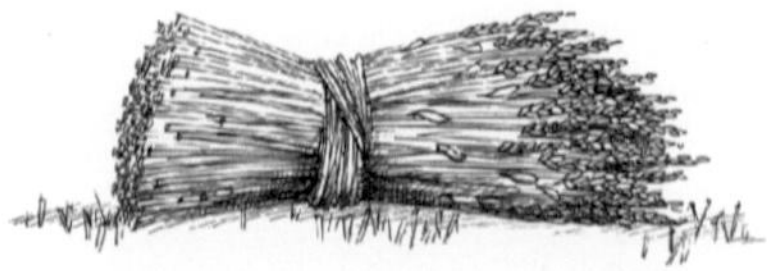

alongside others belonging to his neighbours. Betty dwelt briefly on Dom Edmund's recent adjudication upholding Hugh's right as a married man to graze more animals than one of his neighbours, a bachelor - but put it out of her mind.....the angry altercations had been disturbing, even before they went to the manor court.

She thought instead of the strips ploughed by her dear Tom. Walking with her on the Watling Street, looking north towards the rolling fields of western Leicestershire, he would tell her how that highway drove along a thin corridor of safe land between the hard rocky soils of the hilly ridge on the southwest where began the Arden forest, and the soft lands beside the Anker on the northeast, with Atherstone's three great open fields.

Her thoughts strayed for a moment to Nat the miller's man...a pleasant living he had working on Windmill Hill Field, out towards Witherley. Better perhaps than living off the Alder Mill Field near the Fieldon Bridge.....dirty and little used in winter's wet weather, and over-lively in the clement seasons when merchants stopped to pay a bridge toll on their goods and wares.

Ahead the squat market building was gradually clearing of goods, and traders were sweeping away the debris of the day's activity, at its busiest at this time of year. The harvest in, prosperity for all was at its highest. She marvelled, as always, at the numbers of folk here, buying and selling – from Witherley, and Bentley, and Hartshill......why, some from as far away as Coventry, Lichfield, even Leicester!

Betty was returned to the present by Dom Edmund's chuckles. She knew him well enough to be ready for the coming re-telling.....the hundred years old story of Alice le Colier and Robert le Taylor, and their fight over a pipe and twelve gallons of wine. The shouts and bustle of the closing market invariably prompted these reminiscences, and the pair shared a ritual enjoyment of the bailiff as raconteur, despite the noisy backdrop.....the packing away of leather goods - harness and shoes and the like, and iron pots and utensils and other kitchenware, and nails and tools, pottery, clothing, the shereman's cloths, wood-fuels (some of it charcoal), livestock, grains and seeds, linen gloves, fruit, honey and wax, game, spice, salt fish, shell fish.

She breathed in the scents and relished yet again the doughty and unexpected actions of coal-dealing Alice. How Dom Edmund wished the trying of these two had been in his court!

"And indeed, sir bailiff, roundly would you have dealt! But come, the coney smells richly, there's good ale. And well have you dealt this day. Frankpledge, frankpledge, there's a weary day gone by for you, come indoors and take your rest....."

NOTES TO CHAPTER 3

This chapter's information on the fifteenth century administration of a small town such as Atherstone has been supplied by Andrew Watkins, and by Marion Alexander. I have also drawn from Andrew Watkins's paper: *Small Towns in the Forest of Arden in the 15th Century,* Dugdale Society Occasional Papers No. 38, 1998.

Alan F. Cook provided geographical and agricultural information.

Although Dom Edmund the man is fictional, the role of bailiff is not.

The local government of Atherstone was administered through the manor court, which comprised two distinct courts: the View of Frankpledge, and the 'Little Courts'. The View of Frankpledge met twice a year, and the Little Court once a month.

The View of Frankpledge originated in Anglo-Saxon times. The vill was divided into tithings (groups of ten men) who were bound to stand surety for the others' good behaviour. It was a collective responsibility to ensure the communal field system was efficiently run and neighbours behaved. It met twice a year and enabled the community to deal with breaches of the strip system and minor offences: regulating victuallers, enforcing rudimentary sanitary regulations, punishing sharp commercial practice, and reporting and punishing violence. Calling upon long held practices and local memory, the community of Atherstone passed ordinances and made byelaws to regulate all aspects of town life. The court carried out its responsibility for enforcing law and order through the officers called constables and tithingmen. They had to report crimes and apprehend law breakers.

Much inspiration for this chapter came from incidents brought before the courts and detailed in the Manor Court Rolls. If you wish to dip into this collection, with its glimpses of everyday life, the following references may be helpful (although be warned: these are in medieval Latin!): Warwick County Record Office Manor Rolls WCRO MR 13/6; WCRO MR13/12; WCRO MR 13/13; WCRO MR 13/15; WCRO MR 13/16.

The copyhold system.

Copyhold, compared to freehold, is an inferior status of landholding. It evolved from the unfree tenure of villeins (with a system of 'tenancy at will' along the way) to a system that was widespread by the sixteenth century (in some instances existing before that).

Atherstone is unusual – and fortunate – in having retained records of copyhold transactions in the Court Rolls from the 14th century to the 19th century. Each time a property changed hands the Manor Court Roll recorded the transaction: from whom, to whom.

The party selling was recorded as 'surrendering' the property. The party buying was recorded after the sale as being 'admitted to' the property. The two parties would have negotiated their terms before going to the Manor Court.

This is reflected in Dom Edmund's explanation to Betty: "...they were negotiating his share of the house before going together, Hugh and himself, to finalise the matter in the manor court. There Hugh would sell a share to Dom Edmund, and Dom Edmund would be recorded as the new owner."

However, although the parties bought and sold, the ultimate ownership still rested with the lord of the manor, to whom the buyer had to pay a fee, also recorded in the Manor Court Rolls. Dom Edmund explains the hierarchy: "The monarch is the ultimate land holder. He gives lands to his lords and vassals in exchange, usually, for money and a fighting force. Likewise then these lords give lands to their tenants in exchange for services on the land and availability as part of a body of fighting men." He also notes, however, that in Atherstone the 'usual' transaction of land exchanged for money plus services was reduced to money alone: "Here in Atherstone the lord's main interest has ever been for the good folk to ply their trades so that the town may thrive." As remarked in the Notes to Chapter 2, "a burgess, although not necessarily free of all manorial servitudes, nevertheless did hold the land on which he had his house by a tenure

sufficiently free to enable him to pursue....economic activities." (Beresford; see reference in Notes to Chapter 2)
Dom Edmund also throws light on the term *copyholder*. "Folk pay their...fees to the lord...and the details of these exchanges of property are all inscribed by me [the court official] in these rolls [the Manor Court Rolls]. People take away their own copy of the manorial record....hence the name '**copy**hold'."
Copyhold tenure was only finally abolished in 1926.

Dom Edmund's explanation of the copyhold system is important and something you may wish to keep in mind as you read later chapters. (For instance in Chapter 6, where it will help you make sense of Dudley Baxter's conversation with Richard Pipes, also of Nathaniel Gimley's post as clerk to the Manor Court).

The importance of Atherstone's Manor Court Rolls.

Atherstone's fortunate circumstance of having records of copyhold transactions in the Manor Court Rolls not only allows us to know of the parties directly involved in property transfers, but also to know of the owners and/or occupiers of the adjoining properties. Very often occupations are given, sometimes with family connections and incidental detail. Sometimes wills are recited. (See also Introduction, page 12)

Betty and Dom Edmund walk from an imagined inn, perhaps somewhere near the site of today's Old Swan, along the south side of what Betty and her bailiff would know as Watling Street (our Long Street), until they cross the road opposite our Church Street, and enter the market place.

The marl pit, or marl pool, was on the hill, on the same side as the present-day Devereux Court and just a little beyond that towards Mancetter. We know that "horses and other beasts of the town" drank from it; for instance, WCRO MR 13/13 reveals that in 1420 one Agnes Parker was charged with endangering animal welfare by putting lime "into a pit called le Marleputt".

Penny prick was a children's game, the object of which was to hit a penny hanging from a string.

Alice le Colier's dispute with Robert le Taylor in 1370 is noted by Andrew Watkins.

<u>Some fictional dates.</u>

It is quite satisfying, and possible, to imagine that Betty's great-great-great-great-grandfather could have been Hubert the scrivener, had he chosen to put an end to his journeyings and settle in Atherstone.

1420 Birth of Betty's father.
Birth of Dom Edmund.
1442 Birth of Betty.
1458 Betty marries Tom, and their daughter Elizabeth is born.
Tom and Elizabeth die this same year.
1462 Dom Edmund, aged 42, comes to Atherstone.
Betty is 20.
(This is the same year that Edward IV gives the manor to Mount Grace Priory.)
1477 The year of our story. Betty is 35.

CHAPTER 4

NATIONAL EVENTS			LOCAL EVENTS
	1500		
Henry VIII	1509		
Dissolution of the monasteries	1536		Dissolution of the Austin Friary in Atherstone
		1546	Henry VIII gives Manor of Atherstone to Henry, Marquis of Dorset
Edward VI	1547		
		1554	Sir William Devereux now lord of the Manor
Elizabeth I	1558		
		1563	Michael Drayton born
William Shakespeare born	1564		
		1573	Queen Elizabeth School founded
		1584	**Dick Simcott's useful day**
Defeat of the Spanish Armada	1588		
	1600		
James I	1603		

DICK SIMCOTT'S ATHERSTONE

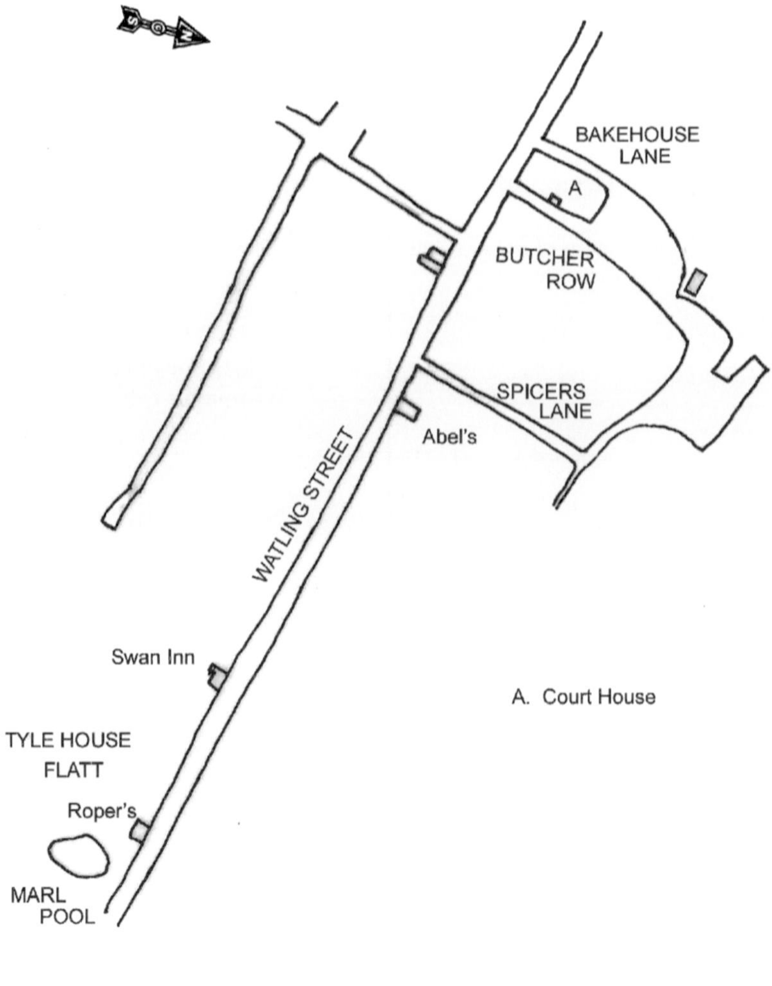

CHAPTER 4

DICK SIMCOTT

1584

Dick Simcott and his family are the only fictional characters in this chapter.

The usual morning cacophony had begun: cocks crowed, cattle lowed, pails clattered, the clop of horses hooves approached and receded. Scattering the straw around him, Dick sat up sharply. His mother was gathering his mewling baby sister to the breast, the while shoving with her feet an empty wooden bucket towards him. "Dickon, my son. Go fetch the water, there's my boy." His three brothers, like small puppies in the hay, rustled and snuffled, reluctantly meeting the day.

With a yawn and a stretch he was up, once again taking upon his thirteen year old shoulders the responsibilities of the man of the house.

Today as yet they had no bread. They had eaten but husks yesterday, and Dick was resolved this day to better that. For as long as he could remember, his days had been focused on earning however much was needed that year, that month, that day, to prise from Bakehouse Lane the vital stuff that sustained his fatherless family. And for as long as he could remember, bad harvests had meant the necessary amount had been rising. So, he had his plan for today – well, a plan to start with, anyway.

But first, water from the nearby market-place pump. Lugging back the full bucket in one hand and clutching a turnip luckily fallen from a cart in the other, Dick stooped to re-enter the shadowy hovel built as a lean-to against the Chantry barn. Alongside, his mother's three chickens clucked and pecked in the long grass of the friary, fallen to ruin ever since the old king had ordered its dissolution

"I'm away then, mother," he called.

"There's my boy. Now forget not my flax stems from weaver Preston. My store is almost worked. There's my brave boy. Go well"

Already John Rampton was harnessing his horse to the horse mill close to their door. The stone cross in the market place cast a long morning shadow that reached almost to the whipping post. Perhaps later that day it would be occupied by some sorry vagabond, for, unusually, the lady of the manor was herself about to preside over her monthly Small Court. Dick hoped not. (He much preferred to see miscreants hunched in the stocks, three folk in a row.....now that *was* fun to behold.)

However, to work. If he did his job well, it might become a regular task – sweeping out the court house and scouring its steps ready for the important business of the day, attended by the senior townsfolk as jurymen, and of course the steward himself, serving Lady Jane Devereux, lady of the manor and widow of Sir William. So, to find his besom, and to work. Which he did, with thoroughness, until, almost done, he reached the outer steps.

"Holla! Dick, my bully boy! Holla there!"

Startled, he whirled around.

"Dickon! Alas the day! Is it not a sorry day? What's to be done? I fear the end of this day; 'twill be my undoing. Aye me...."

Like a single bundle of unruly, flapping, somewhat stinking clothes the agitated person of Alice Dreiton presented herself at his shoulder, shedding grimy fragments onto the cleaned flagstones.

"Dick, dear heart. I'm before the court this day. All for my jollity in delighting good folk with the playing of games in my house.....surely the good Lord cannot gainsay a little laughter with the dice. And I'm charged with brewing illegally, and not for the first time. Well, well; for the sixth time, but let that be. But I feel there may yet be help for me, for am I not good kin of Master Thomas Drayton? Oh, he has no word for me when we pass on the Watling, yet his father and my father were cousins - of a kind, so said *my* father anyway - and I warrant he thinks the shame of one Drayton is the shame of all Draytons. So if I were put to endure the stocks...."

"Good Alice, what's this to me? A poor step-sweeper, how can I possibly ease your plight?"

"My hearty boy, you are young and fresh-faced. Go and speak for me at the house of Thomas Drayton. Ask him to make my case for me in court. And here for you...," her voice took on a wheedling tone, "....here is something for you to spend"

Dick viewed the dull glint of the lead token and needed no further inducement. Securing it in the little pouch at his waist, stacking away his broom, promising Alice his best endeavours, off he raced.

Dick's flying feet took him swiftly down Butcher Row, dodging a couple of cows tied up outside the common butchery where preparations were already underway for what would be their public dispatch.

Turning into Long Street, racing beneath jettied upper storeys of timbered houses flanking its pot-holed surface, he was soon before the imposingly solid door of Thomas Drayton, yeoman. He had paused, daunted by its authority, unsure what to do next, when a small glass-paned window was flung open.

“How now, sirrah! What do you here?”

The sharp-voiced speaker was none other than Thomas Drayton himself, a leather doublet thrown over his flaxen shirt.

Dick gathered himself. “Give your worship good morrow. I bring a humble plea from your kinswoman Alice. She begs, sir.....”

“Fie, fie. Alice, eh? Best come in and tell all”

Stepping over Master Drayton’s threshold first into a passage, then through to his wooden floored hall, Dick felt intimidated. Through the window he glimpsed a kitchen across the yard, where pans hung from pothooks above a wood fire. He even spied a brass kettle! Out of the corner of his eye he spotted a door ajar at the end of the hall that offered a glimpse of a smaller room, fire-lit.

Only too aware of the tumbling hugger-mugger ways of his own one-roomed existence, he felt too awkward to gaze around boldly, but nevertheless took in the large table in the centre of the room, upon

which were several plates...and they were of pewter, not the wooden 'treen' ware. A red stone pot for Thomas's beer stood beside them. There were two chairs; Dick could not help but notice their turned legs, and, even more dazzling – their green silk cushions. He registered a cupboard against one wall, upon it a thick green cover, and a brass candlestick whose candle was but recently extinguished, to judge from the lingering beeswax smell. (No tallow here in a Drayton house.) And upon another wall - Dick thought he had never seen anything so fine, not even in Mancetter Church - was a painted cloth showing herbs, and beasts, and knots.

His shy sightseeing was curtailed as Master Drayton recalled him to his errand, which Dick recounted as best he could, trying to keep faith with his pay mistress Alice. His account failed to move her prosperous - and distant – kinsman.

"Go to, boy. I'll not be seen to hold with her capers. Why, I needs must think of my own dear Alice, my good wife. Nothing shall tarnish her name, nor indeed her father's name, brave Thomas Nutt, faithful neighbour that he is."

Dick could not hide his disappointment. The wealthy man of affairs - butcher, tanner, shoemaker and town elder - had turned away, leaving him to move towards the door.

"Wait, fellow. I'll warrant you'll not say no to running an errand for me? There's a pair of shoes to be delivered for me to Master Abel. Here's a token for your pains." Dick felt a flash of pleasure. "And what's more," added his new paymaster, "he's a juryman today in court, so you can lay Alice's cares on him."

Long Street was fully awake now, folk spilling from the fifty or more properties that crowded together along each side. Dick knew that other folk would be toiling on the long narrow strips of land behind the buildings. The sun was strong on his face as he nimbly wove his way round two gossiping alewomen, flagons temporarily rested at their feet. He neatly avoided Master Rawlatt the chandler, canvas-wrapped bundle under his arm. He held his breath to block out the stench from Peter Tompson's fish cart. He ducked in and out of a gaggle of labourers shouldering their spades. Past pewterer, haberdasher, plumber, glazier, nailer, tiler, ropemaker - it seemed to Dick the town's whole population was in his way. He dodged the creaking

wheels of a miller's overloaded cart, noting ruefully the gift of spattered mud and dung he received from them. He saw with relief that he had managed to protect the shoes destined for good John Abel. He would not for the world present Master Abel with anything but the sweetest. A protector of the poor must be himself protected.

Here now was Spicers Lane. Here close at hand was the Abel house - a scene of great busyness.

Shielding his eyes, Dick looked aloft to where John Weston was precariously astride one bare roof beam, deftly applying his carpenter's skills as he drove in the peg to fix it to the post.

"Save you, master" called Dick.

"Faith, save thee, friend" returned the craftsman from his high perch, and began to scramble down. Dick had chance to appraise the numerous additions to the old one-roomed house that had belonged to an earlier John Abel, grandfather of the blacksmith John that Dick knew and admired. How the place grew!

John Weston caught his approving survey.
"Aye, my gallant. You're seeing the mansion house Master Abel plans. There'll be eleven rooms in all, think of that. See, the old house stays as the parlour. Now then, round it we're to have - mark ye well - a hall, buttery, kitchen, nether parlour...."

"A parlour and a *nether* parlour!"

"Even so. And all with a chamber over. And a shop, a kiln house and a malt house, which Master Abel considers perhaps should not be annexed under the same roof as the house.....he is fearful of fire, as to be sure are all of us dwelling in these woody houses. But let them not be so far distant but that the good man lying in his bed may easily hear what is doing in each of them and quickly get help if needed."
The carpenter broke off to shout an instruction to one of several workers busily unburdening a cart of its load of tiles. "Holla, good Benjamin! When done, pray give the day over to care of my beasts. For my gentle Buttercup cries to be milked, and my pigs and hens must be fed"

He returned to Dick, explaining, "Here be seven good men and true, well versed in the ways of the fields, who'd be standing before Lady Jane belittled as rogues and vagabonds were it not for Master Abel's employment. Our wise blacksmith master knows how the land fails them"

His glance fell upon the shoes Dick held. "What brings you to his door?"

Dick's account, covering both shoe-delivery and frantic Alice, was quickly grasped by the practical carpenter.

"Peace, then, sir Dick. Now listen well. I will be your messenger on both counts when Master Abel calls back, in the midday halt to the court's proceedings, as her ladyship ordains. Trust me, I'll speak heartily. Meanwhile, do you go up the hill towards Mancetter and find Thomas Roper's brick 'n' tile works up there on Tyle House Flatt, near the marl pool, and tell him we need one more cartload just like the one we had this morn."

Dick nodded.

"Are ye hungry, boy?"

Dick nodded more vigorously. The carpenter reached behind the half-built wall and fished out a hunk of bread and half an onion.

"Sit and eat, my lad. Take a panikin of water. Then ye can race about again"

Thus fortified, and in short time, Dick was away, loping down, then up, the inclines of the highway that some still called Watling Street. He had no difficulty in finding Master Roper's works just before the marl pit. No one could miss the frequent rumbling carts, some ox-drawn, plying in and out; the smells of the plumes of smoke rising from the kilns. 'Thomas Tiler' was growing rich, all the town knew it; 'Roofer Roper' was ever in demand, what with the need to cram more houses onto the thin corridor of land on which Atherstone stood, and the fire-safe law that forbade at Pain[12] any work beneath a thatched or wooden roof after dark. Candles could quarrel with thatch or wood.

---

[12] penalty imposed by the manor court on townspeople who disobeyed what were, in effect, byelaws.

Dodging past a couple of men unloading a cartload of shale from the Outwoods destined for Atherstone roofs, Dick balanced his way gingerly along a plank laid over the sucking, clayey path to Master Roper's shop door. The tiler could be seen beyond, blackened up to his knees with dust from the intervening serried range of recently burnt-out kilns. He barely looked round, occupied as he was with supervising a couple of sweat-drenched workers who were carving out a pit as base for the next kiln to come into production. Dick's message had to compete with the clatter of a lad's stacking of a barrow with new-made flooring tiles, now cooled and hard and ready to go. Thomas Roper responded brusquely with a mere nod.

Then as an afterthought: "You going back down the Watling, boy? Into town? Do ye know old Master Nutt?"

He rummaged in the dark depths of his workshop. "Take him this one slate.....'tis long promised since the storms of last month. One slate's too little to be carted. But with care, do ye mind. No falling, brawling, somersaulting or slackness. Do it well, and here's a token for your pains"

Dick caught his breath with delight, eagerly stowing away his third payment of the day. A loaf of bread formed in his mind's eye, three little pairs of hands outstretched. And with a "thank you, honest gentleman," he was away once more.

Rich old Thomas Nutt was ill. He had been ill for many months now. If ever he did appear, in his customary seat at the sign of the Angel in the market place, people shook their heads behind his back to see his shrinking frame and lined face. This day his son Edward opened the door of their one-roomed house, ready to dismiss Dick once he had taken the promised slate from him. But the old man's voice quavered its thin request.

"Let me see the boy"

Thomas lay nested in a deep feather mattress, a flaxen sheet between him and the heap of hilleys and twillies piled over him for warmth.

“Lay across me that coverlid, lad,” said the sick man, pointing to a tapestry-worked counterpane, followed by an unexpected chuckle. “Never as a boy did I think I’d have pillows at my head. Only for women in childbed, so they said then. Why, my father used but a good round log! And look - here’s a new thing – me on a bedstead! Heh, heh....the world goes on. Things are marvellously altered. Chimneys! What a multitude of chimneys of late. When I was a lad there were not above two or three in all the town.”

His weak laughter turned into a bout of coughing.

“I need ale,” he mustered. “I want you to go to Alice Dreiton and fetch me some ale. Alice brews ale as I like it.” Dick opened his mouth to tell of Alice’s troubles.

The old man raised a pale hand.
“Nay, fear not. Alice is surely most lackadozy......sometimes a Dreiton *is*....why, there’s John Dreiton, common fisher, selling fish illegally, and Hugh Dreiton, making affray again and again....but they have much of their hardworking kinsfolk’s goodness too.” He smiled fondly. “Not that Alice lives up to young Michael, that most learned of her kin, sent away to study, of whom great things will come, I warrant thee. But Alice sits not in the stocks this day. She is in mercy, with four pence to pay. And because I relish her ale, and need her ale, that’s four pence I have paid.”

A surly growl came resentfully from Edward in the doorway, but the invalid ignored it.
“You’re a good fellow, Dick my heart, and I trust you. So take this purse to Alice, bring me my ale, and” - he fumbled under his pillow, “here’s a silver halfpenny for you.”

With the fleet arithmetic that comes from dire need, Dick saw that the coveted coin took him to his day’s target, and much further. He would secure his mother’s next supply of flax. But more, with pride he would return home bearing bread! And, and, mmm, perhaps beans, too!

Tomorrow he would........he would....

.....Whatever it was he would, off went Dick Simcott to do it, that day as every day energetically spinning his life across the little town.

NOTES TO CHAPTER 4

Information in this chapter comes in the main from Marion Alexander, based on research on wills and inventories held at the Lichfield Record Office, and wills in The National Archive. Marion also supplied information on entries in the Parish Register.

Alan F. Cook gave invaluable information on tile-making, and roofing, and Nat Alcock provided guidance on several other points.

Some details of domestic life were provided by *Documents in English Economic History 1000-1760* H.E.S. Fisher and A.R.J. Jurica, published by G.Bell and Sons Ltd., 1977.

Bill Grimke-Drayton's collection of Drayton family records, compiled in 1994 (unpublished), gave much useful information.

I took the names of the townspeople crowding the street from records of Views of Frankpledge (in Warwick Record Office).

I have placed Dick in an imaginary hovel built as a lean-to against a barn on former Friary land, on the north side of the market place, a little further north than the present-day church. My choice is based on the 1547 survey (WCRO L2/8) which shows that after the Dissolution the Chantry in sum held three and three-quarter burgages, the three-quarters being divided into two houses and a barn.

Dick's mother is carrying out work for weaver Preston that may have involved preparing flax stems by removing their woody waste. She would have to 'ret' it - soak it in water - very smelly & unpopular - then break it, afterwards combing it, to leave the long linen fibres that were to be spun. A William Preston appears in records in the parish register as having been left 'loome and geres' in his father's will, which suggests he could have been working at the time of this chapter.

John Rampton, whose family is known to have had a horse mill, is mentioned in the Manor Roll for 1590. The 1547 survey shows him as having two mills, both a water mill and a horse mill.

A Court Hall is recorded in the market place in 1547, between Christopher Dreiton's barn and a shop belonging to John Wilkinson (Drayton records; see above).

Sir William Devereux died in 1579, after which his widow Lady Jane acted in his stead as 'lord' of the manor. I encountered some initial difficulty in understanding her role in 1584, mistakenly believing her husband still to be alive. My mistake was based on Watt and Winyard's *History of Atherstone* (page 17) which gives Sir William's death as 1589. I alert readers to this typographical error.

Alice Dreiton [sic] appears frequently in the records of View of Frankpledge around the time of this chapter. She sells goods illegally, she makes excessive profit, she does a little illegal baking, she conducts illicit brewing operations, and, her crime here, she "illegally plays games in her house."

The sites of the houses of Thomas Drayton and Thomas Nutt are imagined.

Thomas Drayton did indeed take an Alice Nutt to wife (Drayton family records, see above). Moreover, the Manor Court Rolls show that Thomas Nutt and his wife Alice surrendered (sold) their property to an Edward Nutt in 1584, who died in 1593 (Edward's will provides the date). I have not allowed old Thomas's wife Alice to make an entry into my tale; but I am crediting a likely daughter, Alice - a daughter with the mother's name - as the wife to my Thomas Drayton.

Spicers Lane (which later became Dog Lane) is the former name of today's Ratcliffe Road. John Abel's house was on its corner, somewhere near where the HSBC building now stands.

You may track references to Roper's property through Chapters 5 and 6.

The tokens that Dick collected were trade tokens, an unofficial currency that took the place of small denomination coinage. Made of lead, they were small and dumpy, and would bear letters or designs identifying merchants, or inns, or trades. Such tokens became rather more frequent in the 17th century.

CHAPTER 5

NATIONAL EVENTS			LOCAL EVENTS
	1600		
		1624	George Fox born
Charles I	1625		
		1633	Death of Richard Warwick
		1641	Plague year in Atherstone
		1641	Civil War skirmishes along the Watling Street
		1646	Death of Hester Warwick
Charles I executed The Commonwealth	1649		
		1656	Dugdale's Antiquities of Warwickshire
Charles II	1660		
Fire of London	1666		Severe winter freeze in the Midlands
		1673	Tilly sitting in the orchard
William III and Mary II	1688		
	1700		

TILLY'S ATHERSTONE

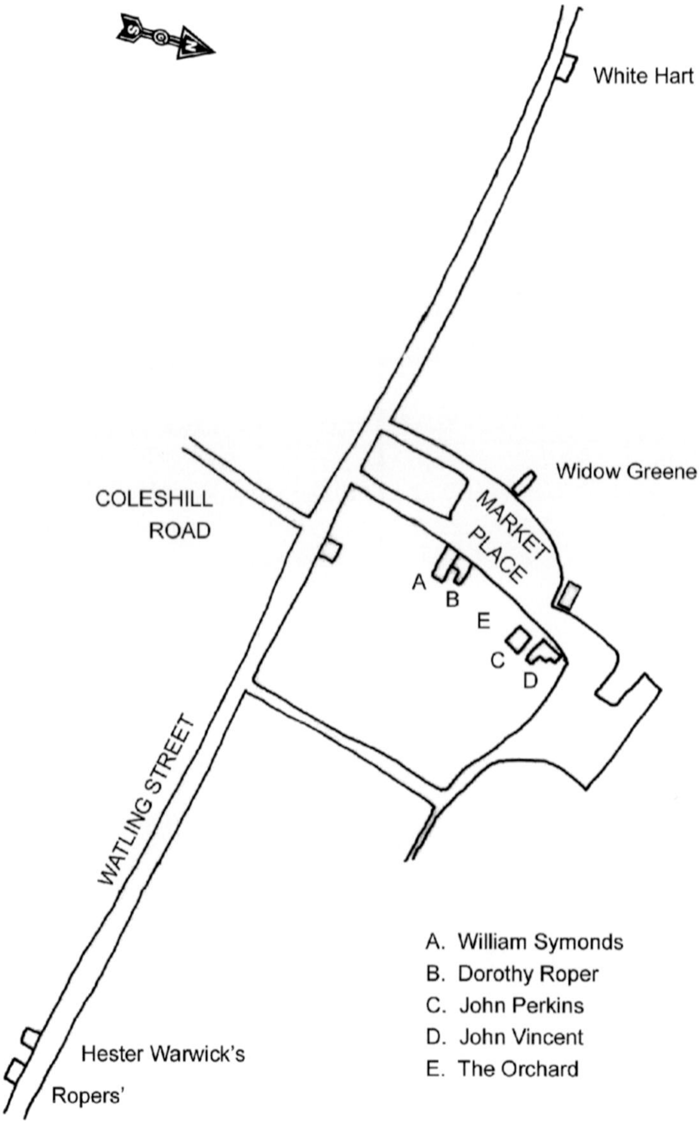

CHAPTER 5

TILLY

1673

Anne Partridge's husband Joseph and her daughter Tilly are the only fictional characters in this chapter.

It was a Sabbath day, a peaceful day. Tilly sat under the apple blossom, sunning herself. A few early bees, roused by the spring sunshine, busied themselves around the hive. Head bent over her sewing, she hummed a little tune.

From across the grassy patch, shaded from the breeze by the tall, thick hedge, Anne regarded her daughter fondly. Twenty-three years old! Almost as old as she herself had been on the awesome day that brought an end to the protected years she had spent serving the Warwick household. Despite the warm sun, she grew chill recalling the dark time of Hester Warwick's last illness.

"Come, Anne...." In her mind she heard the deep and serious tones of William Symonds exhorting her to ignore her trembling hands and witness with a cross her dear mistress's last will and testament. With Elizabeth Higham's arm around her shoulders and Hester's pale but unwavering smile to encourage her, she had made her mark. Mr. Symonds had read to her the lines: *I do give and bequeath to my trusty servant Anne Partridge the sum of three pounds in money, with my mohair petticoat.....* (she still wore it) *....and my safeguard and hood,* and Anne had seen in Hester's dimming eyes an overflowing of thanks for twelve years of devoted care.

Not many years before, together they had pulled through black days when plague came and culled so many others. A dark year - they had barred the doors when news reached them of skirmishes on the Watling Street nearby, brothers for the King fighting even their own brothers if their swords were raised for Parliament. And the following year Hester and Ann had listened ashen-faced to accounts of Caldecote's siege. Even nearer to hand, in their own parish, there was the cruelly random death of poor Anne Averie, accidentally slain by a piece shot. Mistress and maid had wept together.

"With my poor Richard so many years gone from me, God knows I'm glad for your kindness," Hester had said. Anne saw then how much she was needed by this lady, frail, yet as active a benefactress as ever. Anne felt grateful that Joseph, her own good man, had known it too, and waited to wed her.

Because the great house Hester inhabited took so much care. Up on the hill, the windmill visible from its back windows, with only the Ropers' house and tile-house between it and the marl pool, its whole burgage of land stretched as far as the Back Way. Such work to keep all clean and neat, such journeying down to the market for Hester's provisions, such baking and roasting and broiling for Hester's generosity to her frequent visitors – not to mention the sturdy beggars who presented themselves at her kitchen door.

Then there were the frequent messages Anne must carry to the fine houses just up from Butcher Row in the Market Place, two houses that belonged to Hester and whose occupants required her attention – sober-suited mercer William Symonds, and John Sutton the barber who had struggled with his potions and unguents to help Hester at the end. It was on those errands that Anne could steal moments with her Joseph, if he was tending what they had called 'their' garden. Secluded behind Hester's two houses, it was this self-same plot where now she sat with Tilly in the sun.

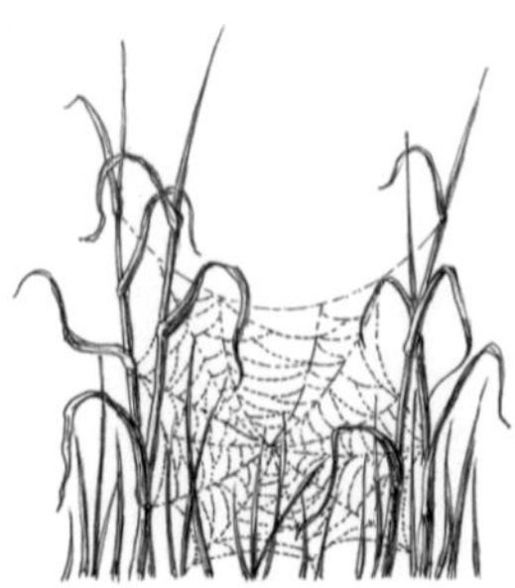

She smiled at the memories.

A cobweb between the grasses caught Tilly's eye. She put words to her quiet humming:-

A cobweb over them they throw
To shield the wind if it should blow
Charles had taught her those words about Queen Mab's attendants.
Four nimble gnats the horses were
Their harnesses of gossamer....
He had told her it was a song Michael Drayton wrote, the same Michael Drayton who was Mr. Harrington Drayton's kinsman and who went off to London and never came back. Charles reminded her that his own great uncle, Richard Warwick, Hester's husband, had been once a citizen of London. Charles said London was wonderful.

She looked up through the apple tree to the topmost branches.

She remembered Charles sitting aloft, lord of the small orchard. "Catch, butterfingers," he had teased, tossing in a slow arc ripe apples for her to catch in her pinafore. "They're *my* apples, but I'll let you have some." He'd be about ten years old then, thought Tilly - always laughing, leaping, climbing, finding new things to do. And I would have been about nine, yes, because I can hear him singing as he hurled one more apple:
This one's for Cromwell buried and dead,
They've planted an apple tree over his head

Meanwhile Anne was remembering apple tarts. And quince jellies, syllabubs, quaking puddings, raised pies, jugged hare, marzipan, chickens cooked with rosewater, raspberries, a collar of brawn, a grand sallet[13] of red bib lettuce with dill, and chives, and nasturtium flowers, surrounded by blanched almonds and sliced lemons. Hester's great oak board had fairly creaked beneath the funeral spread.

A few days before that Anne had been trimming the lanterns when she'd overheard Mr. Symonds tut-tutting in his deep, ponderous voice: "So, Mistress Warwick distributes a mere five pounds to the poor but commands a glorious ten pounds for funeral bread - and wine - and cakes...." Anne herself almost burst out in defence, ready to cite Hester's countless kind acts and plentiful gifts, not to mention the great heart that had willed her final act on this earth be one of joy and celebration. Luckily, Anne was kept from that by the intervention of Reverend Richard Abel. She heard him quietly wondering whether to quote Master Shakespeare in his funeral sermon: *Dost thou think, because thou art virtuous, there shall be no more cakes and ale?*

So cakes and ale it was. Hester's hall was crowded, wall-to-wall. Her brother Charles Careswell had left his merchant tailoring in London to be there with his wife Zipporah and his daughter, beloved of Hester and named after her. There were others from London, too. (Anne had worked hard into the night, for Hester's sake, to make a spread suitable for such fine folk.) Good neighbour Anne Barnes, a former Widow Roper, was delighted to see her sons the brothers Roper again at home - John the London blacksmith and citizen Abel the stationer.

Dorothy Roper their kinswoman was there, having crossed the town from her house in the Market Place next to the one John Sutton occupied. He was there too, conferring gravely with Samuel Barrow the apothecary. John Vincent, who lived at the top end of the Market Place next to the schoolmaster left his wife Anna talking with her Roper family, and sought out Harrington Drayton. Harrington had a young gentleman in tow, one Edward Hinton. Anne thought it strange

---

[13] salad

that a fifteen-year old should spend more time looking around the house and lands than at the funeral board.

Little Elizabeth Ison grew more and more tearful the more she partook of the wine. She lived in a tiny cottage in the corner of Hester's yard against the Watling Street, where her husband Henry had plied his feltmaker's craft. Her tears were for Henry and Hester both, she confided to young Richard Wilday, seeking sympathy from one who, a few houses further down the Long Street, shared her late husband's trade.

George Wightman, who ran the White Hart at the far end of town, thoughtfully sipped more wine, gazing at his new wife Elizabeth.

Mr. Symonds had managed to overcome his earlier reservations about the funeral meats, tasting judiciously, the while in earnest, bookish conversation with Mr. William Clare and Mr. John Perkins. He declared himself pleased with a recently acquired volume "Farmers alarum to drowsy saints". Mr. Clare envied him this, owning six books himself but ever wishful of more. John Perkins was silent; though schoolmaster, his library was but small. William's son John Symonds looked on, then turned to proffer help to Anne, in difficulties with a new wine cask. For which he'd sensibly slipped away to fetch an iron lever from his house at the bottom of Long Street's slope.

Hester's kinsfolk Thomas Hodgkins and sister Mary Davies took a little time outside to inspect the Ison's small cottage: Mary grew thoughtful about its merits. Widow Goodruff Gligham made sure the company appreciated the fullness of the bequest Hester made her. "Two blankets! Two! Yet did she stay her hand at blankets? Faith, no! Now my old bones rest on a flock bed. God bless Mistress Warwick." With which Granny Gligham reached for another pickled cucumber.

Then, from across the miles, there had come news that an end to the fighting at Oxford seemed like to end the war. Hester had been a lady of peaceful ways. It was fitting.

Tilly was born into peace, mused Anne. How peaceful she looked now, she thought, watching the gentle rhythmic rise and fall of her needle in the dappled orchard sunlight.

"Can I remember a time when I didn't know Charles?" wondered Tilly silently. It wasn't just the little orchard that held his memory. The whole space had been her childhood playground, because her father Joseph not only managed the fruit trees but also gardened the small-holding and managed the twelve-foot long square of land once used as an ash pit, (upon which he later built an up-to-date 'house of office'). The hedge, high and thick around this L-shaped enclosure, bounded for her a place of contentment. It had always seemed her secret garden, where the hurly-burly sounds of the market place were muffled, the lowing and squeals from Butcher Row grew faint, and busy Long Street's many brick-built inns and shops and houses were securely shut out. The way in was hidden inside the gatehouse in the yard that belonged to Mr. Power's big house - people called it his mansion house. Power's land stretched so far back from his Long Street house that it met the lands behind Mistress Warwick's Market Place houses, the ones that later became Charles's.

Tilly looked around her, reflecting fondly on how large a kingdom it had seemed to her childhood self.

In and out the beanpoles, in between the onion sets, into the hovel where father kept his tools and the apples were spread out to dry and where she often saw the whisk of a receding rat's tail. And she had shared all this with Charles. *He* said he shared it with *her*. She came to understand this, as she grew.

Sometimes he would take her hand and they'd go visiting.

They went to see Widow Greene who lived in Mr. Symond's house on the other side of the Market Place, and she gave them strawberries from her garden.

Once they went to see Anne Draper in the tavern on their side of the Market Place, but she was swabbing the stony floor, and Thomas her husband was rolling barrels in from the buttery, and they shouted at them to get out.

Once they went to the Swan, close beside that tavern. John Hall was dozing, and they giggled because his feet were dangerously close to the embers of the fire. So they peeked at the long table and stools and cushions in the diners' parlour, and crept from the hall with its three tables, forms and more stools, into the rather more fine yellow walled chamber with one little table, a form, a coffer and, grandly, a chair. Charles put his finger to his lips, and they even tiptoed upstairs, sneaking a little slice from the corner of a half-cheese alongside sacks of malt and oats in a storeroom. But she shook her head at his whispered suggestion that they continue down to the wine cellars, despite the temptation, he said, of French wine.

Well, was there ever a time when she didn't know Charles? Of course not, he was born the year before her. He may even have seen her first tottering steps.

Anne shifted out of the sun's glare to sit beside Tilly, approving her needlecraft.

A score of years dissolved in her memory, and she saw in her mind's eye her infant daughter under the apple trees faltering towards a young Charles, himself still unsteady in his steps, still befrocked....Master Charles, object of his parents' doting affection.

Anne recalled her pleasure on hearing that young Hester Careswell had married Thomas Wells, a London merchant tailor no less. Her father's trade connections had proved advantageous. Her aunt Hester would have been delighted. So, some three years on from the famous funeral feast, Master Charles Wells made his debut in this world. She remembered how loudly he used to cry. Master Charles was ever demanding. Unlike his gentle mother.

After old Hester died, the Market Place properties went to her brother Charles, and Zipporah. For some four years they would visit Atherstone as often as was necessary to supervise their properties. There was much to remind them of London's unsavouriness. Tanning bestowed on the town its own peculiar compound of distasteful smells.

Butchers consigned unwanted gifts of bloody offal and fragments of hide to the streets. Nevertheless, Charles and Zipporah found it preferable to London. They appreciated the strenuous efforts the town made, by exacting severe fines through its system of Pains[14], to reduce these nuisances. Each time, they returned reluctantly to the harsher dangers of the disease-laden streets of the capital.

And each time they returned to the smoke-palled city they found the health of their young Hester ever more frail.

Eventually they grabbed the opportunity to take over the garden....this sunlit spot...behind their Market Place properties. And next, when they had the chance, they returned to occupy the house that had been Dorothy Roper's. For young Hester this proved an escape route from her struggle with the malodorous streets of London. It was a great relief to her to stay with her parents....bringing with her little Charles.

Anne had found more than employment with this family; she also found a boy child who needed her sensible care. It had worked well, she reflected - happy years of Charles and Tilly playing together as she got on with her tasks. The London death of his father Thomas cast a shadow, of course it did; Hester's spirits never recovered. How swiftly she weakened!

Anne sighed, recalling the day she had had to find the children in the orchard, draw them to her sides, and with an arm around each little waist tell Charles he had a mother no more.

[14] penalties imposed by the manor court on townspeople who disobeyed what were, in effect, byelaws.

Tilly was silently considering. It was under this tree, she believed, under this tree then heavy with fruit, that they heard Charles's mother was dead. Her own good mother had left them here together. Charles lay on his back, looking at the blue sky, laced with thin clouds. He said they were like cobwebs. There was a little breeze to flutter the leaves. Charles said he would always remember that day. She said the same.

Yes, they did go on playing together, but it was never the same. Charles was truly master now, because his late mother had inherited the Market Place houses from her parents (his grandparents), and now it was his turn: he inherited them. And more. He inherited their secret garden.

"Coming, Tilly?" he would invite. "Coming with me into *my* garden?"

Tilly smiled to herself as she remembered how she could coax him out of such boasting – for a while. But he began to spend more and more time in London. His grandmother Zipporah was his guardian, and she wanted to put a London gloss on him, wanted his education broadened from what Mr. Perkin's school in the chancel could provide.

There were still lovely times in the orchard when Charles was spending time back with his grandparents, and he would regale Tilly with accounts of the way London folks lived. He used to visit Mr. Abel Roper at his bookshop in Fleet Street. (He spoke admiringly of Abel's daughter Susannah). He spent time with John Alsop, citizen and scrivener, and with Thomas and Lettice Loveday. They all had some connection with the Ropers, of course, and first Alsop then the Lovedays took over Dorothy Roper's house. Much more fascinating to Charles was the fact that Mr. Loveday was a goldsmith.

In return, Tilly made him laugh with stories of the customers in Healey's shop where she worked....the unceasing procession of buyers for pans, brushes, kettles, knives, candles, and candlesticks.... She'd take a breath, watching his face to see if his interest was maintained.

"......And raisins, alum, aniseed, treacle, sugar, caraway seeds, mace, coriander, nutmeg and pepper. Charles! Listen! Hammers, nails, tar, oil, clogs, gunpowder, beeswax, tobacco...."

"Tobacco, huh? Well, well. But no gold, I daresay, eh, my little Tilly?"

Then when he was sixteen London claimed him as an apprentice. Tilly had feared so for his health that first year, when folks spoke in hushed voices of the ravages of the London plague. Worse was to come next year, when she had to wait all through that severest of winters for news, once she'd heard John Loveday the town crier proclaiming the disaster of London's fire. After that Charles hardly ever visited Atherstone. When he did they were short visits, full of assignments with associates of the Ropers, and the Lovedays, and supervision of his own property.

Charles was apprenticed to a longbow string maker, Robert Hill, who also became his guardian. Tilly was proud of the choice. Using a longbow called for great strength. Charles had told her that drawing the bowstring back to his cheekbone was the equivalent of lifting a big sack of potatoes with just two fingers.

Tilly knew an apprentice was bound for seven years. She imagined his life amongst the industrious merchants of Cheapside. She had heard that the houses were so close in the narrow streets that apprentices in the garrets could shake hands across the way. On May Days she thought of them escaping to the countryside for the day. She heard of the playhouses on the south bank of London's great river, but thought Charles was probably too busy to attend. She thought the making of longbow strings would be immensely complex.

She turned with satisfaction to show a neatly finished seam to her mother.

Anne thought: I believe my girl is content these days.

She had seen a calmer Tilly since last year when John Symonds, Mr. William's son, came to tell them of his meeting with Master Charles. On his father's behalf John had conducted the meeting well, rescuing Charles from financial difficulties with a loan of £30 against the properties.

It was good that Mr. William owned Charles's houses now. He had asked Anne to stay in service, and Joseph to husband the land; their quiet sojourns in this walled spot could continue.

A man of few words, John had little to say about the Black Bull in Cheapside where the deal was effected.

"Full of smoke, ma'am. Noisome. Sweaty-capped musicians. Brisk boys. Loud."
He turned then to Tilly.
"Charles asked me to give you this."

He handed her a paper.

"Printed by Mr. Roper. Written by Michael Drayton. Charles said it would remind you of a day, once."

Anne saw Tilly 's cheeks redden.

"If it please you, sir, I cannot read it."

It was John's turn to colour. Unfolding the paper, he read:-
Clear had the day been from the dawn
All checkered was the sky,
Thin clouds like scarves of cobweb lawn
Veiled Heaven's most glorious eye.
The wind had no more strength than this,
That leisurely it blew,
To make one leaf the next to kiss
That closely by it grew.

“Tilly,” said John, “Charles told me he says to you, ‘goodbye’.”

Anne dwelt on John’s straightforward, honest sympathy as he looked on Tilly’s tears.

Tilly sewed on. She was thinking of the same.

NOTES TO CHAPTER 5

Much information in this chapter again comes from Marion Alexander's research on wills and inventories held at the Lichfield Record Office, and wills in The National Archive.

Hester Warwick's will of 1646 was the start-point for the reminiscences of her "trusty servant" Anne Partridge.

Alan F. Cook, Nat Alcock and Val Pickard provided guidance on several points.

The Manor Court Rolls (see Notes to Chapter 3) provide the names, occupations, circumstances and residences of the Atherstone townsfolk in this chapter.

Charles Wells's story is taken from this source, (WCRO L2/14, L2/15, L2/16).

A most valuable aid to the realisation of the town inhabited by Anne, Tilly and Charles is a map produced by Judy Vero. Judy has tentatively derived this from the important map of 1786 (see below). Using information from the Manor Court Rolls, she has been able to replace the 18th century inhabitants with their predecessors, thus providing detailed information on the town's 17th century inhabitants and where they lived. However, this work is in its early stages and is not as yet definitive.

The 1786 map of Atherstone

The 1786 map has been central to the researches of the H.A.R.T. It shows as still discernible the boundaries of those ancient burgages allocated by the Abbot of Bec in the 13th century. It gives all the properties along Long Street and around the Market Place, and names each owner. It allocates a number to each property, and indicates whether it is freehold or copyhold. (For 'copyhold', see Dom Edmund's explanation to Betty in Chapter 3, and my notes to Chapter

3). Now using these numbers, it is possible to provide the locations of many of the properties in this chapter.

There are 2 copies of the map at Warwick Record Office (WCRO P26 and CR2511/21). Several other copies exist, one being with Atherstone Town Council.

"The great house Hester Warwick inhabited... up on the hill" stood approximately on the site of present day Regal Court. Hester's property extended to the Back Way, that is, to today's South Street. It occupied the site of C54 on the 1786 map. This is a site that you may track through later chapters.

Richard Warwick's tomb stands grandly in the churchyard of Mancetter Church, near the church door.

Butcher Row is the former name of Market Street.

The houses in the Market Place that Hester owned, and which eventually passed to Charles Wells, are today numbers 15 and 17 Market Street, between the former Church's restaurant and Beech House. They are C100 and C102 on the 1786 map.

Tilly's garden with the apple trees was somewhere behind today's Beech House

The description of the interior of the Swan is based on a description supplied by Judy Vero from the *Torrington Diaries*, 1789, Hon. John Byng, Eyre and Spottiswood, 1935 Vol II, page 97.

'The tavern in the Market Place was on the site of today's Market Tavern'

The landlady is swabbing a 'stony' floor. The adjective is deliberate: the floor may have been solidly embedded cobbles, or flagstones; in default of definitive evidence I've abandoned the lady to her engagement with something rather vague!

A chronology for the characters in this story
(conjectural and fictional dates asterisked)

1621* Anne Partridge born.
1634* Anne Partridge aged 13 begins work as Hester Warwick's live-in maid
1646 Hester Warwick dies. *Anne Partridge is 25.
1649* Anne Partridge marries Joseph.
1649 Charles Wells is born.
1650* Tilly is born
1658 Charles Wells's father Thomas dies.
1659 Charles Wells's mother Hester dies.
1665 Charles aged sixteen apprenticed in London. *Tilly is fifteen.
1672 Charles's apprenticeship ends; he is 23.
1672 Charles Wells and John Simmonds meet in Cheapside

(Sometime in the 1670s John's father William Simmonds establishes a dissenters' meeting house)

CHAPTER 6

NATIONAL EVENTS			LOCAL EVENTS
	1700		
George I	1714		Newcomen Engine installed at Griff
		1724	Daniel Defoe makes reference to Atherstone's cheese market
		1728	Samuel Hinton, father of Fleetwood Hinton, buys the house formerly Hester Warwick's
George III	1760		
		1761	Watling Street and Coleshill Road turnpiked
		1763	Act of Enclosure for Atherstone
		1768	Cutting of the Coventry Canal
		1778	Benjamin Harris builds Thomas & Theodosia Hear's house
French Revolution	1789		
		1790	**Thomas Hear spends the day chasing Theodosia**
		1798	Diversion of Sheepy Road through Swan Entry
	1800		

THOMAS HEAR'S ATHERSTONE

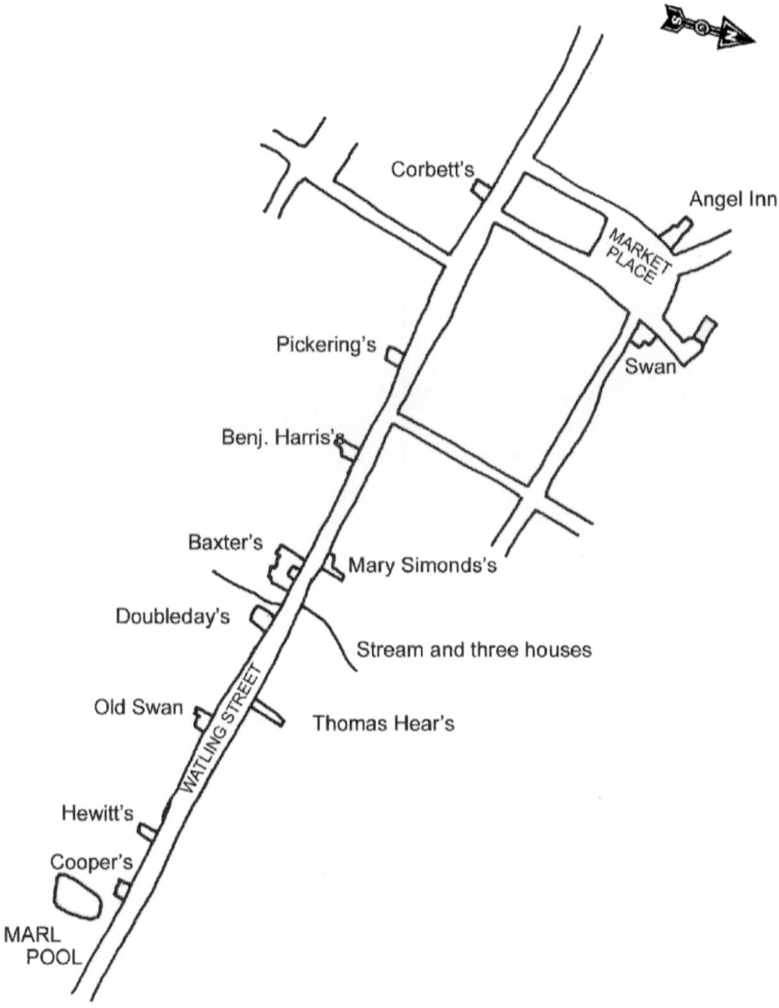

CHAPTER 6

CHASING THEODOSIA

1790

The only fictional characters in this chapter are Simcott the tanner's apprentice; Deborah, serving maid in the Wilday household; and Nathaniel Gimley, clerk to the Manor Court

So much to do, so very much to do. Hesitating outside his house across from the Old Swan, Thomas Hear rubbed a work-hardened fist across his forehead, his small features pinched with anxiety. He glanced up at the lowering clouds.

He ought to be down Long Street, calling in on his five houses for rents already two weeks overdue. Theodosia had reminded him only that morning, when she was trying to decide between her red velvet tippet and her green. Nor had he as yet visited his Long Street ribbon workshop to have last week's weaving loaded onto the packhorses and sent off to Coventry. As for his business in plumbing and glazing....How was he to concentrate on anything at all when he knew not where Theodosia had spent her day?

Was Theodosia content?

Would his wife *ever* be content?

He had thought he could make her so, when first they married. He had trusted his dashing new bride when she told him a plumber made a fine man in her eyes. And she said she admired glaziers above all. They were strolling close to Mr. Bracebridge's Hall at the time. He sensed that Theodosia felt she belonged on the other side of the wall.

Soon afterwards, here on the very spot where now he stood (and rain threatened), she had watched the builder Benjamin Harris take down three old houses ready to put two new ones in their place - pulling off roof tiles – pushing out daub panels in vast clouds of dust – heaving down framed walls to the great danger of life and limb and adjoining property. These houses were special, for the usual practice was to demolish in order to *increase* housing, not reduce it.

So from that moment on she gave Thomas no peace. It was "Thomas, we must have one. So close to the Baxters! Thomas, I might become acquainted with Mrs. Sarah Baxter. She calls on the Bracebridges. We must live on the hill. Thomas, I wish to take tea with the Misses Hinton. We shall be quite across the road from them. Thomas, Thomas..."

The careworn little plumber remembered. All through the winter of seventy-seven to seventy-eight there was Theodosia in the wet and the wind, stalking the building site and giving her orders, forever changing her mind as to which of the two fine new houses suited her best.

Eventually she rejected the house next door. That was taken by the Reverend Christopher Preston, to *his* great comfort. For Reverend Preston had confided to Thomas, man to man, that he found it very difficult to share a necessary-house with the exacting Mrs. Vincent. (She had occupied the cellars and kitchen and room above where he lived previously, in the Market Place.) Thomas recalled the detail of the good Reverend's house, so very similar to his own: *Extending in front twenty-one feet towards the street, with brew house, coalhouse and other offices, and garden staked out beside it extending backwards from the necessary house thirty six yards, and courtyards, walls, ditches....* Necessary-house! Such refinement! Theodosia had been pleased, then.

A bout of coughing racked his thin frame. He turned up his coat collar. He must find her.

His musing had taken him further up the hill. Across the road a woman stood on the far side of the marl pool, flanked by two children whose hands she clasped. She seemed not to see Thomas. She gazed across the pool towards the house on its western bank. He recognised Mrs. Edmund Cooper, with young Fleetwood and little daughter Frances.

Something about her stillness kept him from hailing her.

Frances Cooper, nee Hinton, was lost in thought. Atherstone was no longer her home. Yet even now, eight years since leaving, she sometimes had to pinch herself to realise she was a Frankton yeoman's wife.

"He's very strong on 'yeoman' when introducing himself," went Frances's thoughts, "reciting to all and sundry that he has forty shillings per annum solely from his own land, his own freehold land. Well, well, I certainly recall the marriage settlement. My father had wide spread properties. Fleetwood Hinton was a prosperous man. He owned places in Lancashire and Northamptonshire and elsewhere, and a deal of land hereabouts, in Mancetter and Witherley and Hartshill. Parcels of land through which the canal was cut; he did well from that, as did all the landowners along its course."

What's more, her father came of an important line. His grandfather was Doctor Samuel Hinton of Lichfield - was he the bishop? - he had books, oh, a quantity of books. He was strong in those dangerous years when King and country fought. "Furthermore," pursued Frances inwardly, "my great-grandmother, his wife, was a rich woman in her own right. Yes, a well-to-do family: witness the property - *Hinton* property - across the Pool before me now."

Frances dwelt for a moment on the fact that the big house once was Richard Warwick's – the Richard who rested in the great tomb beside Mancetter church door. Later, it had come to her father Fleetwood from his father Samuel, who'd had it from his brother Edmund Hinton (to Edmund's great sadness he remained childless).

"Mama, may we walk on now?"
Frances was brought back to the grey-clouded October present. She looked down at her own children beside her, and squeezed their hands.
"Soon, my chickabiddies, soon."
Her children sensed the pressure of memories, and stayed compliant for the moment.

Frances recalled that, like Edmund Hinton, Richard and Hester Warwick were also afflicted by childlessness. Surely, she convinced herself, the house is unlucky, and its misfortune has various shapes.

She rehearsed the sadnesses of her own young life in the house. She lost her father when a child, and, when still only girl, her mother too. And in the same year in which she grieved that loss, she began to lose her sight: it became a year of twin misfortunes, hard to endure. Around that time her elder sister Barbara married Charles Hewitt, and the house became theirs. Frances remembered the day. She faced the festivities all wan and forlorn, her only support the arm of her good, kind relative Hester Hinton.

Hester, ensconced for the purpose in the little cottage tucked into the Hewitt's grounds beside the Watling, gave Frances the love her guardian found impossible to give. Frances acknowledged the Reverend Thomas Clare's good intentions; but he never could unbend to take the place of the parents she missed so dearly. Faced with her terror at approaching blindness he could only speak stiffly of "your unhappy situation regarding your sight".

But many other people did try, in so many ways, to improve her condition. When Mr. Seager in his Market Place house had tried and failed, Benjamin Harris consulted his business friend Thomas Turner, also an apothecary. He came all the way from Oxford, yet his physick had no effect. Good neighbour Robert Lingard wrote to a druggist in Smithfield, one William Cooke, but even a London chemist had no remedy.

Then they had found her a pair of spectacles. And she refused to step outside, dreading the laughter of strangers and children. "Come," would say her guardian Thomas Clare, "you have your own pew in both churches left you in your mother's will. What have you to fear in such journeys?" But she would only creep to Hester's chimney corner to struggle with her embroidery in the shadows. "No-one will marry me" was her plaint, and indeed that seemed like to be true.

"I overlooked my wealth," thought Frances, a trifle bitterly. "I forgot about my lands. A prosperous father is able to provide for daughters as well as sons. Barbara had the big house, I the smaller one between hers and the marl pool. And shares in all the lands, both far and near." Her gaze took in the orchards, gardens, and little, well-tended plots stretching from the pool to the Back Way.

"Sometimes," she recalled, "a man stipulates in his will that a woman's inheritance is for her use and hers alone, and never a husband may use it."

Indeed, her own husband Edmund had recently scoffed at one, a Mr. Lawson, who in 1771 ensured that his daughter Mary's annuity would not *be subject to debts or control of her present or any future husband.*

"Wise man," reflected Frances ruefully. "More's the pity my father did not so. Yeoman Cooper has bitten hard into my wealth."

She sighed, remembering how slowly she had come back into the light, slowly recovering her sight sufficiently to read, write, and answer all common purposes of life – how that happened no one quite knew. Slowly she had blossomed. She had been so happy to go off to Frankton with her bridegroom.

"Edmund thought he understood the clever property deals of others around him, like brother-in-law Hewitt, who benefited from passing his house to the Reverend Thomas Clare. But my yeoman Cooper is no Hewitt, or Harris, or Baxter, or Bracebridge."

Her eyes rested again on her former house.

"The house that was mine is a Hinton house no more. My fine husband's traded it to a Coventry gentleman for an enormous sum......." She counted the figure, to the penny. "£1267.4s.4d.........a gigantic sum.......with interest. His study of commerce was sadly inadequate; sadly for me."

Frances glanced down at her son, who was glumly kicking a pebble from one foot to the other.

"But *not,* I determine, sadly for my boy. I'll work against that. My Edmund Fleetwood Hinton Cooper – proudly named! I'll find the resolve and the art to defend his future!

"So, my dears," she declared, rousing herself, "let's away to London now, and find our living there."

The children's spirits lifted, and all three laughed as, dancing, they spun her around.

On coming to rest she found herself facing a deferential Thomas Hear.

"Miss Hinton, ma'am. Er..." He corrected himself. "Your pardon, ma'am, Mrs. Cooper. Please, ma'am, I'm anxious to know, excuse me, I'm anxious to find my Theodosia. Have you seen her?"

"Oh, Theodosia of the rich dark hair?" She was laughing still. Then regret resurfaced.

"No, Mr. Hear, perhaps you've forgotten: Atherstone is no longer my home. I have not seen her these last eight years."

She turned away, winding an arm around each child.

With a stammered "beg pardon," and a mumbled "God be with you," Thomas, embarrassed, eased himself away.

A few steps further towards the town, questions about his wife's whereabouts once again kindled his strength of purpose. It could not be right for their daughter Sara to be burdened all alone with household cares, and she a mere lass of fifteen. Sara should be learning housewifery at her mother's side. He pressed on, ignoring alike the spattering raindrops and his own rasping cough.

Rumbling sounds of rolling barrels came from over a yard wall on his left, accompanied by shouted instructions and yells of " 'Ware!" Having passed the Old Swan, the large timbered inn which Mr.

Bracebridge owned, (though never stooping to *work* there, of course), Thomas now stood beside Robert Lingard's property. A malty, mellow smell softened the late afternoon chill. His good friend Lingard was at his maltster's trade. So: he wasn't required today as Manor Court juror, or experienced will-maker or attorney. But best not interrupt him; his thriving brewhouses kept more than one Atherstone inn in good supply, very necessary what with market days, and thirsty Watling Street travellers clamouring as they alighted from their coaches, and all. Anyway, Theodosia wouldn't have spent any time in a maltster's yard.

By now his steps had taken him to the next premises down from Lingard's - old Doubleday's house and tannery, on the other side of which rose Dudley Baxter's mansion.

He had to pick his way even more carefully at this point because a little brook flowed out from the tannery to run across the road, where it converted the spot at which it disappeared into a minor quagmire. The water ran oily brown. It gave off a pungent smell that told of Doubleday's oozing tan pits co-existing with mounds of poultry droppings collected to soften the skins. Thomas was grateful for the little bridge that took him across. Three little houses had once sat beside it. But Mr. Dudley Baxter had felt inconvenienced by them – no matter to him that they had long been ideal for skinners and tanners – so down came all.

Theodosia had not been sorry to see them go. She hated all tannery stench. "Yet inordinately fond of her white kid gloves," Thomas thoughtfully noted to himself. So Theodosia had supported the Baxters in such moves.

She said as much to Doubleday's wife Ann, when Ann related the tanner's tussle with Dudley. "My Robert," narrated Ann, "went to court to ensure my tenure of our property against the day that he departs this life – may God forbid as yet. And didn't we hear the law laid down! You see, in the past my Robert, or maybe his father, they somehow got to build a kiln that jutted into neighbour Baxter's grounds. Mr. Michael Baxter it was then, he responded by clamping a wall round all forty-eight square yards of it! So in court Mr. Dudley most fiercely laid claim to that very wall! We were not to have the wall! Around our own kiln! Not even its foundation that runs under our garden.....not even *the drip of the said wall and all the privileges therewith*! That's how you prosper, you see....claim your foundations and relinquish not one drip of your wall."

In his mind Thomas replayed Theodosia's toss of the head as she turned her back on Ann. The picture re-fuelled his need to find her. Someone in Doubleday's works might know; the town's tanners bought hides from the town's butchers, and Daniel Swann was a butcher.....

The thought of Daniel Swann made him draw a long breath, then squaring his slight shoulders he turned back to push through Doubleday's cluttered gateway. Its arch was almost filled by a cartful of oak bark brought down from the Outwoods to be powdered then layered with skins laid flat in the water-filled tan pits. The forest scent was momentarily refreshing.

He didn't recognise the worker acting as beam-man, bent over his

wooden post, with rhythmic strokes shaving smooth one of the lighter hides. One more newcomer to the town, he realised. So many newcomers.... so few places to build. Land all round the town, for sure, but none for homes. But Thomas recollected himself sharply. Such was not his present concern.

He pressed further into the premises. From the far side of a heap of fresh cowhides Mr. Doubleday's kindly voice could be heard offering tuition to his apprentice:
"Now d'ye see, young Simcott, first thing's to get rid of all the flesh as is adhering to these. Yes, yes, filth, to be sure, but d'ye see....."

Thomas knew he must ask what he'd come to ask. "Robert, good man, God give ye good day."

Leather apron to his ankles, Robert Doubleday stepped out into the open.
"Ah, Thomas! How goes the world today?"

"Busy, busy," muttered Thomas as preamble. Then straight to the point:
"I wonder where Theodosia has spent this day. Have you seen her?"

Immediately he knew it wasn't a sensible query.

The elderly tanner respected his predicament, and replied gently that he lacked information on that point.
Then young Simcott piped up.
"Daniel Swann delivered these hides this morning." Doubleday shook his head warningly at the boy, leaving Thomas to wheel sharply about and make for the gate.

Head down, he collided with Joseph Corbett. Relief flooded through him. Here was a trusted confidant.

Joseph assessed the strain on his fellow glazier's face. He took Thomas's elbow and guided him into the vacant space where once stood the three little houses on the bridge. Though dampened by drizzle, a fallen beam served them as a bench. With a view to steadying his friend, Joseph began to talk of business.

"Good to see you, Thomas. I couldn't leave the joiner's shop until I'd set up work for that new ward of mine, John. He's sorely missing father John Taylor; good carpenter, very good. I had much work out at Ratcliffe all yesterday, for Mr. Payne." (And, he acknowledged privately, was most happy to do so, for courting of his pretty daughter Mary.)

"But I wanted to talk to you. Hear me. There's property in Long Street you might care to consider. It was Thomas Pickering's, on t'other side of Long Street from Dog Lane. I've heard it might be possible to acquire it. Think on't." He added an encouragement: "Theodosia would be proud to see your holdings increase."

Receiving no reply, he continued: "I've just been making certain arrangements with Benjamin Harris. Now there's a model for us builders, eh? From poor beginnings, by astute and brave dealing, our Mr. Harris flourishes. He long since ceased to style himself mere 'bricklayer'. It's 'mason' now. Well, consider the fine work he's done on the church. Do you know, my friend, I believe he rents out upwards of thirty properties here, *and* others in Nottingham.

"And how did he start? I'll tell you. With that one house of his just along from the Baxter's going towards the Red Lion; his house with the chapel behind it. He set himself up back in 1760 with £380 got by mortgaging it to Thomas Turner....you know, the baker's son turned apothecary. Aye, Harris had to work fifteen years before he'd made enough to reclaim it. And now there's the chapel he's erected behind his house. Perhaps the chapel is a way of saying 'thank you' for the start the house gave him.

"That's where I've just been - at the chapel measuring up for him. How do lawyers put it? *All the necessary easements, roads, ways, paths and passages to the chapel as well as from Long Street as from the back road.* Benjamin stipulates nothing more may be built there, save perhaps in future a wall. James helped me today, his son. Bright fellow. He had us using a pear tree and an apple tree as markers to measure from. Says these specifics are vital for will making. Looking ahead of himself, that young man!" He chuckled.

Thomas's expression had grown increasingly purposeful as Corbett expounded.

"You touch on a concern of mine," he said. "I want your help to draw up my will. No, hear me." He raised a restraining palm at Joseph's protest.

Rapidly he explained. "My life is Theodosia's. All I earn and all I own. And when I'm gone it must be, shall be, hers. And she'll marry again. Of course. She will. So here's the nub, Joseph. I'll not have another man take her simply for what she owns. My will must make it clear that what I leave is for her alone. Nothing, *nothing*, for any husband"

"You'll provide for Sara?"

"Aye, Sara too. And to oversee the will, along with you, we'll have young James Harris. Good. We'll see to it then."

He stood as though to leave. But there was one more question he had to ask.

"He's doing well, is he, Daniel Swann, butcher from Birmingham?"

"Not that well, Thomas my friend. Still sharing another's butchery space, still lodging in a tiny tenement out behind my casting shop." (And looks the dandy despite sharing the one pump, thought Joseph, but kept that to himself.) The two men shook hands in shared understanding.

Thomas stepped out into the road, already gamy with horse droppings and now filled with a drove of cattle heading eastward. He scarcely noticed their lowing and their steamy breath, their herdsmen's shouts; he fought off a fit of coughing and turned towards the town.

But wait! Perhaps Theodosia had again tried to call on Mrs. Sarah Baxter. Although he'd passed the Baxter mansion he halted, wondering whether to go back and attempt a query.

Then he heard Dudley Baxter's loud tones ringing confidently from somewhere within the higgledy-piggledy complex of dwellings people still referred to as Old Mills's: three small back tenements behind the front dwelling, cramped together with stables, sheds, storehouses, gardens, grass-ground, and its own little well. Mr. Baxter was haranguing Richard Pipes who lived there, though he made his living running the wharf beside the canal at the foot of the Coleshill road.

And an increasingly good living, too, recognised Thomas, thinking of the opening that summer of the link to Fazeley that joined Atherstone to the wider canal network. Mr. Pipes daily managed vital exchanges: coal, lime from the local limekilns, limestone, all kinds of building materials....other goods, many and various.... Thomas shook himself; such inventory-making was not his business. He returned his attention to Dudley's tirade.

"Faughhh, man! The Pains[15] of the manor require any pits or wells to be fenced off, and as I can assure you, that should mean pig sties also. But come, have ye given thought to what I proposed last Lady Day? Hmm? Selling your holding here, to me?"
"Mr. Baxter, you have long craved your neighbours' dwellings. Fine additions, sir, to your house, your gardens, orchards, backsides, barns, stables, hovels, and dove houses. But I think we shall stay. I mind old Benjamin Mills. Remember him? Shambling home at the fall of dusk after a day bent over his plots, much of the plots still about his person?"

The curl of Dudley's nose showed he did indeed remember.

"But we both know, sir, the careful will with which the old gardener sought to retain for his four dear children the benefit of his life's labours. He learned from me, Mr. Baxter, not to feel shame that he must close his will with a cross. Many's the good man - and the rich man - who cannot write his name."

Disregarding Dudley's clear suspicion of that statement, he continued:

---

[15] penalties imposed by the manor court on townspeople who disobeyed what were, in effect, byelaws.

"So all was left to his children, and - " Pipes emphasised the quoted words, "*that little room at the end of the stable.* He left that little room to his precious granddaughter *for her to enjoy for ever* - Elizabeth, Elizabeth Wilson - yes, so light and dainty and her with a collier father!"

Eavesdropping despite himself, Thomas was forced to raise a smile at Pipes's assertiveness. He even imagined that Baxter may have become a little shamefaced, especially at Pipes's next thrust.

"Yet only this April, fearing herself slipping from this world, gentle Elizabeth sold you that same little room over the stable, and even her fourth part of the very grass around it. She's away to Coventry, poor soul, her parents dead and no husband. She waits still for the Jervis lad from the White Hart, who left our shores for fortune in foreign parts. Who knows for certain whether he be living or dead? In France maybe, where all is turbulence now, or America, where they fought to be free."

Thomas could imagine Dudley's well-worn recital that would follow: how his father Michael had acquired the little toft across the road that had been Howson's Yard, and how his brother got the tumbled down cottage next to it, where once lived William Bailey, feltmaker, with his son the horse-rider. And all these now were Dudley's, and how right and proper that was, as was his acquisition of the other Bailey cottage between his mansion and Old Mills's. So it was only right that he should have Mills's land too .....And so on.

Thomas felt it was not a good time to accost him.

The rain fell more steadily. He'd press on to the Market Place. Theodosia may have shopped there. His quickened pace took him swiftly past Harris's house with its apple-treed chapel behind, past the opening of Hall Lane beside the Red Lion, past landlord Joseph Beale sweeping the front of the Three Tuns. He passed the narrow passageway that led to Corbett's casting shop, where it jostled for space among all the other premises crowding a plot stretching back to the pond in Back Way. But Corbett and John Taylor had done a good job: two new Long Street dwellings fronted the yard where once there was but one. He crossed the cattle-bespattered road to traverse Bakehouse Lane into the Market Place. It wasn't a market day. In the darkening afternoon there were few people around. It seemed the only sound was his cough.

A chaise drawing up to Swan House caused a brief commotion, a clatter of hooves, sounds of voices giving orders, greetings. People went inside, the horses were accommodated. Again the square fell silent, and candlelight filled the windows of the unbroken three-bayed façade of Atherstone's most important building. Landlord John Rogers had efficiently bustled in another consignment of Watling Street travellers.

Thomas went to cross the Market Place, thinking to return home, when he noticed two women sheltering under the arch of the Angel yard. His cough told him he should shelter, too.

"Master Thomas, come under here, come out of the rain. This weather's too harsh for you."

His near neighbour Mary Simonds, mother of eight, was chatting with Deborah, one of the serving maids in John Wilday's household. Thomas was glad for their solicitude. To offer good will in return he said, "I saw your eldest today, Mary. He's a strong young worker."

"Indeed," confirmed Deborah. "Today he took on his back one of the hugest padding pokes of wool from my master's hatting shop, to take home for Mary's workers...."

"...me, and my man, and my own children." interposed Mary. "We're the workers" (Thomas was only too familiar with the smells from Mary's bason shop[16] behind her house.) "And once we've hardened that load, why, back again it goes to Wilday's, my Edmund again bent double under it all the way down Long Street. Ah, the boy...he jests:

---

[16] where the wool receives its initial compacting, or hardening (Vero, *A Concern in Trade,* Warwickshire Books 1995. page 84)

'seems like going all the way to Tamworth, mother!' But thanks be, I can trust him to bring back our pay. "

"Oh, John Wilday pays," conceded Deborah. Then she confided: "He's thinking of a new invention – a *machine* to do the carding! He might set it up in Leathermill Lane."

The three contemplated a mechanised future.

"How fares little Joseph?" asked Mary of her serving-maid companion, knowing Deborah's affection for her master's youngest son.

"Five years old, and a true little Wilday. Can't get enough of his father's machines!" Deborah laughed indulgently. "And very fond of his prayers," she added.

Thomas remembered his quest. "Has Theodosia passed this way?"

The two women exchanged a glance.

"Master Thomas," Mary advised, "Nathaniel Gimley has news you may appreciate."

Nathaniel Gimley was the long-serving clerk to the Manor Court of Atherstone, and it was but a moment's walk for Thomas to the door of his secure little cottage.

Within, Nathaniel Gimley had just lowered his tall frame into the high-backed chair at his fireside, after giving another stir to the pan of mulled wine. He drew appreciatively on his clay pipe. It had been a long day. He gazed around his little room with satisfaction, snug as it was, with clean wainscoting and matted floor. A clock made by Mr. John Pinchbeck ticked its secure tick above the fire. On the oaken settle across the hearth sat the small bespectacled figure of William Thorley, rotund in white waistcoat and cream pantaloons, his damp outdoor cloak flung across the back.

"Well, well, William. Let's be hearing how fares the pawnbroker's trade. But first, Mr. Thorley, a pipe and a sup?"

Nathaniel passed over a pipe already filled, and William bent to light it at the little wax candle that stood before them.

"An overture to conversation and friendship, Mr. Gimley", he returned, on receiving his measure of hot, spicy wine.

Firelit wreaths of smoke wove around the two men. The little candle sputtered in a draught.

Their reverie was disturbed by Thomas's tap at the door. "Lift the latch, friend, and come in," called Nathaniel.

So bidden, Thomas entered, shaking the persistent October rain from his greatcoat, accepting gratefully Nathaniel's invitation to be seated.

Before Thomas could frame his question, Nathaniel launched straight in. "We hear much, William and I."

The pawnbroker nodded gravely. Court business and money business kept these two well informed.

Nathaniel continued: “We know Daniel Swann is looking to open his own butcher’s shop. He’s skilled at his trade; it should do well.”

If the big, raw-boned, red-headed fellow can just knuckle down, thought Thomas privately.

William elaborated the point. “If he were to take a wife, she’d have cushions to sit on”

Thomas’s cough shook his thin shoulders.

“Come,” proffered Nathaniel, “drink with us.”

“We’ll set Atherstone to rights,” said William Thorley.

A log on the fire settled lower upon its glowing bed of coals, sending up a sprinkling of sparks. William sucked on his pipe. “There’s money for you in the painting trade,” he opined.

Thomas looked into the dancing flames, and he could see his future.

NOTES TO CHAPTER 6

Judy Vero and Marion Alexander provided much incidental information for this chapter, while Alan F. Cook and Nat Alcock both gave valuable guidance on many points.

Information on leather working came from *Illustrations of Useful Arts and Manufactures* by Charles Tomkinson (London 1858), supplied by Judy Vero; with further information from inventories supplied by Marion Alexander.

Important sources of information for this chapter are the Manor Court Rolls (see Notes to Chapter 3). From here are drawn the names, occupations, circumstances and residences of the Atherstone townsfolk who feature in Thomas Hear's life.

And it is here in the 18th century that these Court Rolls really begin to offer an absolute wealth of detail that present a great many possible starting points for stories. Selection proved very hard.

Observant readers will note variations between chapters in the spelling of the Simonds family name, appearing also as Symonds and Simonds; the spellings reflect entries in the Manor Court Rolls. (Just as the Draytons also appear as Dreitons, in Chapter 4).

As in the previous chapter, this chapter includes some of the history of certain houses and the sites upon which they stand. These now relate directly to the 1786 map: WCRO P26 and CR2511/21 (See notes in Introduction, page 12).

Because some readers may find opportunity to refer to this map, the following list uses the map's property numbers. But for use without that map, the list also gives some present day reference points:-

- The two houses Harris rebuilt where there had been three were C71 and C72. The Hears had C72. It stood in the gap to the north-west of today's Black Horse, at approximately today's 152/154 Long Street. The Rev. Christopher Preston takes C71, but by 1787 he is dead, his widow Mary Preston continuing in the house.

- Before that (from 1775 to 1778) the Rev. Preston had shared with a Miss Vincent in C100 in the Market Place. Now 15 and 17 Market Street.
- The Baxters were in C44 (today's Conservative Club).
- The Misses Hinton were in C54, which of course was on the site of Hester Warwick's 'great house' of Chapter 5, a site which becomes the workhouse in Chapter 7, and is approximately the present day Regal Court. After Barbara Hinton's marriage to Hewitt, Hewitt sells C54 to Rev. Thomas Clare.
- Hester Hinton was in F13 (the little Ison cottage of Chapter 5). The site occupied a little section of the front right-hand corner of today's Regal Court.
- Frances Hinton inherited C55; the 1786 map shows it as her husband's, Edmund Cooper's. It was formerly the Ropers' (which links back to 'Roofer Roper' of Chapter 4). It was approximately on the site of today's Devereux Court.
- The Doubledays were in C45, (where nowadays stands the Atherstone Garage), next to the Baxters.
- From 1654 until 1770 there is record of "three little houses on the bridge" between C45 and C44, until a 1793 record tells of "a vacancy where houses formerly stood". Exactly where the 18th century bridge was placed remains a matter for conjecture. However, there are existing oral accounts of this brook as flowing over the road, in a ford, where it dissipated into a marshy area. (We are grateful to Clive Orton for this information, which is also confirmed by Dave Atkin)
- Joseph Corbett's joiner's shop was in what will become Bluebell Yard, C22, (see Chapter 7). That is to say, "the narrow passageway that led to Corbett's casting shop" was on the opposite side of Long Street from the Market Place, midway between Market Street and Church Street. This is where Master's bakery is now, nos. 87-89 Long Street
- John Taylor's shop was in Long Street on the west side of the above passageway.

- Pickering's property which later became Thomas Hear's was C32, now 121-123 Long Street
- Benjamin Harris's yard with chapel behind was C36 and was known as the Coach and Horses Yard. It was 137 Long Street, where the Woolpack Way car park stands today, near Garner Canning solicitors.
- The property that was Benjamin Mills's was C42. Elizabeth Wilson's "little room at the end of the stable, for her to enjoy forever" would be somewhere at the top of today's Council House car park, near Woolpack Way.
- The White Hart, placed then as it is now, is at the west end of Long Street on the north side.
- Howson's Yard was C83. Next door, C82 once belonged to William Bailey, "town horse-rider." These two, C82 and C83 were on the site of 124-126 Long Street, where Irvine House stood, next to Denham and Hargrave's hat factory.
- Another Bailey property, acquired by Baxter, was C43, immediately to the west of today's Conservative Club (hence his desiring C42….empire building…)
- The Red Lion, the Three Tuns and Bakehouse Lane of course stood then where they are now.
- In the Market Place stood the Angel, and the Swan (the former offices of Sale, Hill & Davenport and the Old Surgery). The chapter is set prior to the creation of the landmark arch.
- Mary Simonds and family were in what is now the Hat and Beaver, C80, where they also carried out their hatting manufacture, opposite the Baxters.
- The Wildays were in C13, 14, 15, opposite our present day Library.
- I have purposely left the location of Nathaniel Gimley's house vague, as befits a fictional character. William Thorley at one time occupied F13, the little Ison cottage of Chapter 5, and later where Hester Hinton gave comfort to Frances Hinton. As noted above, the site occupied a little section of the front right-hand corner of today's Regal Court.

Frances Cooper (nee Hinton) stood beside the marl pool looking back towards the town, with what had been the Hinton property in front of her, more or less where Devereux Court stands today.

Some of the family history of the Hintons and the Hewitts is to be found on memorials in Mancetter Church.

Frances Hinton was under 21 at the time of her marriage in 1780/81. She was perhaps about 11 when her father died, about 19 in 1774 when her mother died. The "unhappy situation as to her eyesight" is recorded in 1773.

Theodosia married Thomas Hear sometime around 1773. They moved into C71 in 1787, where they had seven years together before Thomas's death in 1794. He is described then as a painter.

Theodosia married Daniel Swann in 1795.

When William Thorley welcomes Nathaniel Gimley's proffered pipe he is quoting Joseph Addison – "Lighting a Man's Pipe at the same Candle is looked upon among Brother Smoakers as an Overture to Conversation and Friendship." (*An History of Tobacco*).

CHAPTER 7

NATIONAL EVENTS			LOCAL EVENTS
	1700		
French Revolution	1789		
		1793	Joseph Corbett marries Mary Payne
	1800		
Abolition of slavery	1807	1807	William Hood buys premises at one side of entry to Blue Bell Yard
		1822	The Corbetts buy Theodosia Swann's old house
		1826	Death of Joseph Corbett
		1830	Gas arrives in Atherstone
		1831	Outbreak of Typhus
New Poor Law	1834	1834	Wilday's workers locked out
Victoria	1837		
Irish Potato Famine	1845	1847	Atherstone station opened for passenger traffic
		1848	Atherstone General Board of Health formed
		1850	**Little Jo's last visit to Mary**
	1900		

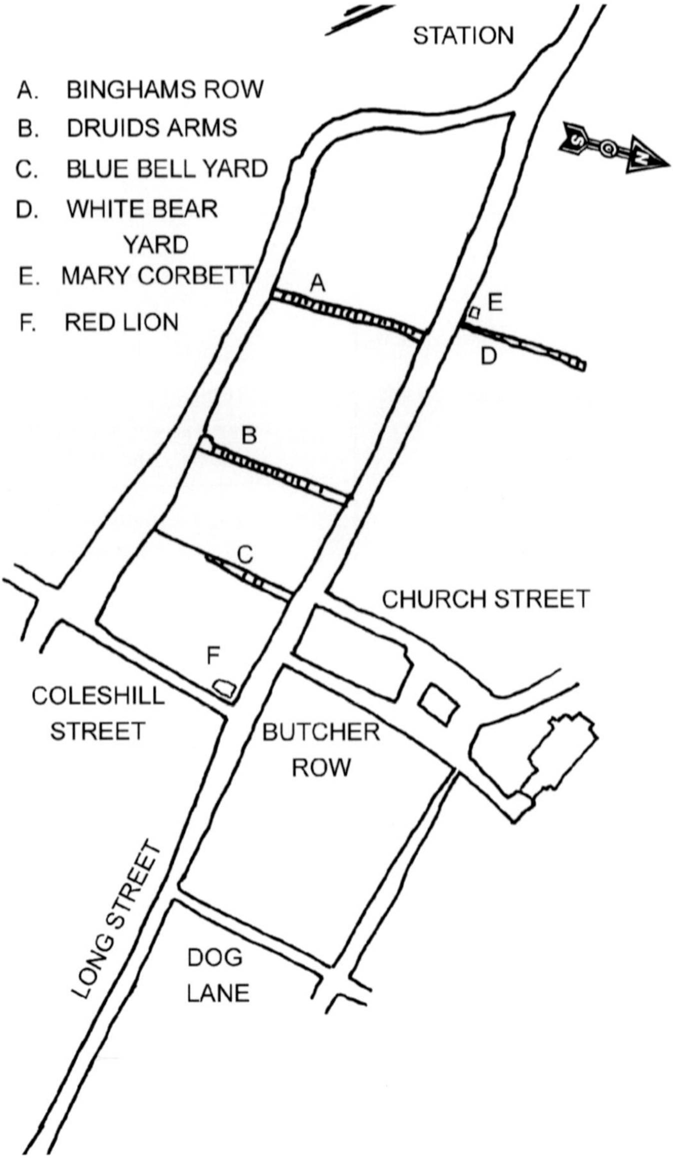
STATION
A. BINGHAMS ROW
B. DRUIDS ARMS
C. BLUE BELL YARD
D. WHITE BEAR YARD
E. MARY CORBETT
F. RED LION
A
E
D
B
C
CHURCH STREET
F
COLESHILL STREET
BUTCHER ROW
LONG STREET
DOG LANE

CHAPTER 7

LITTLE JO

1850

Amos Broadby the tammy weaver is the only fictional character in this chapter.

It was the hooves on the cobbles that woke him, as cart and horse rumbled out of the yard and into Station Street, passing through the entry at the far end. The boy shook off his heavy blankets and scrambled to kneel upright to look out of the small square pane above the bed he shared with his two brothers. Thin April morning light filtered in upon their hunched forms, asleep head to toe. Peering down the length of the yard, Little Jo caught a vanishing glimpse of the painted flowers adorning the tailgate of the Blue Bell's station wagon, away to pick up whatever goods were assigned to it off the six o'clock train.

Up betimes. Good. "Consider the ant, thou sluggard. Consider her ways and be wise," murmured Little Jo to himself, reciting his copybook practice from the day before. Little Jo was no sluggard. And today he had a purpose: to find out more about the Susquehanna letter, the intriguing transatlantic letter from far-away Pennsylvania.

His younger brother Thomas snuffled, and wriggled into the space relinquished by Jo, unwittingly launching his feet (somewhat grimy) into William's face (equally grimy). The twelve-year old grunted and pushed aside the offending limbs. Little Jo, three years his junior, saw it and smiled, for a moment tempted to pounce on the pair and start a joyful rumpus. Then, sensible as ever, he thought of the little ones snuggled in another blanket-heap in the windowless space around the corner of their L-shaped room: his young sisters and - only ever quiet when asleep – the baby. His mother should have some respite.

He kept silent and turned again to the window, as usual enjoying his viewpoint as a special luxury – a window being an asset denied to most yard children accustomed to sleeping in the stair-head space. He leant his elbows on its narrow wooden frame and pressed his forehead on the glass. He could hear the scutter of rats in the loft, the chirp of sparrows in the eaves above.

He was looking down into a long, narrow space, a gully that carved a thin corridor between the overbearing brick walls of dwellings and workshops, made even thinner, for part of its length, by a man-high wall separating the Blue Bell yard from its neighbour. He amused himself with a little calculation: from his window at the Long Street end to the exit in Station Street the yard must be the same length as fifteen or sixteen station carts. Yet only just wide enough to allow the careful passage of one! Here a small wooden shed had been tacked up against a house. There a low wall enclosed a shack that sheltered a communally owned pig. Further along was the stable. Beside that, a shack to house the cart. A pile of Mr. Gretton's felt hoods, left outside to dampen, leant up against scattered wooden blocks. Within a little enclosure a few hens were already awake and scratching the earth. Nothing green, thought Little Jo; green fields and woods all round the town, but nothing green in the yards, except moss in the shadows where the sun couldn't reach.

The yard close behind his father's shop was Blue Bell Yard, named from the public house on the west side of its entry from Long Street; his father's shop was on the other side. His little window afforded him a central vantage point. Jo – who was fond of playing around with letters in his head - thought the shape of the back of his house was like the letter L. The longer stroke of the L was formed by the buildings that hunched along the left side of the yard, as he looked out. His little window looked out from the shorter, lower stroke, and just above the point where the high dividing wall met his house....he had a good view to either side of it. The Blue Bell Yard, however, did not run straight; he couldn't see all the way down because of its slight twist to the right.

"But you don't need to see, to know what's there," thought Joe wryly. "Your nose tells you. One stinking privy for all the yard, with its ash pit beside it, and liquid filth oozing through its walls, and...." he searched his mind for the phrase he had heard Mr. Thomas Corbett use.... *pestiferous gases flowing into the houses.* There was another word, too. He remembered: *miasma.* Mr. Corbett told him that miasma was *exhalations from decaying matter which poison the air.* Little Jo loved the learned words. But he had to live in the stench.

At that moment, as if to underline his thoughts, the Jamieson brothers emerged beneath him, trundling their foul-smelling handcart. The Jamieson brothers were Atherstone's night-soil men, their task being to clear the town's ash pits. Little Jo found the two brothers indistinguishable. Both lived in garments caked with excrement. Both wielded their shovels purposefully. Neither brother was talkative; conversation was rarely required of them, even when purchasing, at a halfpenny per bucket, the yards' collected urine for sale to the tanners, who found it essential to their trade.

The sucking squelch of their labours was followed by the rattle of their stowed shovels.

The early morning sun failed to reach into the yard.

Nevertheless, yard dwellers began to show themselves. Little Jo watched the procession to the pump, which was immediately below him beside the dividing wall. First out was Sam Gisbourne. As postmaster he needed to be at the station to collect from the six o' clock train, and he was running late. Lateness with the post would affect his other duties as constable. Joe saw what he couldn't quite hear: even as he splashed his head and shoulders, Sam directed robust chiding back through an open door to Mrs. Sam and their six children. Jo knew how his words would go. "How can I perform my duties when I have no support from those who depend upon me....."

Next came Richard Gretton's two workmen, joking and jostling each other to bring pails of water back to Gretton's house and impress his daughter with their attentions. Gretton himself would be out soon, thought Jo. He'd need to get the day's hatting work up and running, right there in the yard, adding more smells and noise. There was the fire to be lit under the great kettle to heat the water for planking.[17]

Jo watched then as Sam Gisbourne moved down the yard to bang on his son's door. Jo liked James Gisbourne. What fun they'd had at the young coal heaver's wedding! It more than made up for the hard work of helping James shovel his annual allowance of coal into the space under his stairs, ramming it in and keeping it there with several stout planks. Jo was following with interest the sinking of the new mine shaft at Baxterley. (Though he had only awe for those lads, little older than himself, who daily trudged from Atherstone out to the pits and spent their days in blackest toil.) Perhaps I can catch James tonight, he thought, and he will tell me how deep now that new Stratford shaft has been sunk.

Sam's noisy alarum served also to rouse the Hardings. Joseph Harding, who would be spending his day out in the surrounding farms employing his skill as cow's leech, hawked gratingly and spat into the running gunnel beside the pump, before submitting himself to its bracing ministrations. He staggered back to his family of six bearing two pailsful of, it had to be said, somewhat viscous water.

---

[17] feltmaking

Landlady Sarah Piercey stood in the back doorway of the Blue Bell, rolling up her sleeves, calling her potman from his garret above the tiny brewhouse.

Mary Dutton did not appear. Jo knew that the seventy-year old pauper relied on her grand-daughter – misplaced reliance on a drunkard - and her two lodgers – well-meaning ne'er-do-wells who never rose before midday. He himself would take water to the old lady before he left for school today. He'd found her a strip of blanket, too, for Widow Dutton's under-stairs rarely held sufficient coal. Her black iron range sitting back-to-back with her next-door neighbour's saw little service, save for the one kettle. The two shelves in her tiny pantry space gave home to more spiders than stores. Yard dwellers relied on each other, but Mary Dutton needed much and had little to give. Little Jo marvelled that remembering her in his prayers seemed so far to have kept her from the workhouse.

Soon his mother would ask him to go to the pump for her, (that would give him a chance to douse himself, too) after which his father would want help in unpacking the silks and cottons come in on that morning's train, quality goods for the Joseph Asher drapery emporium, his father's neat shop that fronted Long Street and masked the cramped conditions behind, in which his family lived. For although they were fortunate enough to have a living room, the space had to double as stockroom.

Jo enjoyed the task of arranging shop displays, sometimes allowing the cloths to drape from the shelves in colourful swirls, or setting out rainbow patterns of threads in the bow window. Old Mrs. Corbett had taught him about complementary colours. His father appreciated Jo's skill, especially since he'd had Corbett's carpenters install new fittings, shiny and polished. "Joseph, my boy", he'd said, "we'll not be outdone by the Suttons."

Little Jo was only two when John and Thomas Sutton refurbished their shop opposite, on the corner of Long Street and Butcher Row. Four little houses had had to come down, creating space for the new prestigious linen and woollen shop. The Suttons had invited Mr.

Asher, their rival, to a grand opening, revealing gleaming counters in an interior warmed by more than one grate, some even with coppers. Jo didn't remember, of course, but his father's anxious re-tellings made him feel as though he did.

The thought of his father's new shelves produced in Jo a little kick of delight and anticipation. Not because of the shelves themselves, no. It was because of what fell out from the back of one of the old cupboards that they replaced. He must read it again.

Swiftly he bent down to jiggle away the small section of loose plaster where the wall met the floor, below the window. The letter was still safe in its hidey-hole. He glanced around. His brothers and sisters slept on. (Seven year old Thomas was perilously close to the stair head, but never mind.) No sound came from his parents in their bedroom, adjoining. With a deep breath, he drew out the folded, foreign paper.

My dear Ann, the writer began, *I trust this finds you in as good health as I enjoy here with my dear wife. Though you will know that we suffer a concern for your welfare. Now under these broad Pennsylvanian skies where the winds blow wide and free, we can scarce comprehend the Tight Little Alley that confines your daily life. My pen once again lacks power, my kind friend, to convey the goodness of the land here, in the green circle of Great Bend, in a sweeping loop of the Susquehanna River. I know your good heart, and know you would rejoice to look out, as do we, upon The Endless Mountains. We trust well in William Penn's promise of a free colony to all mankind. And our house is mighty fine. (You smile, I think, to hear the new ways of speech of your Atherstone-born friends?) You would admire our wood panelling, and the painted canvas that covers our floors. But to my theme: my wife reminds me of your aims. Indeed, she urges you to pursue the purchase. Further, she asks me to request your views upon the Recent Discovery which we had the privilege to convey to you, ultimo.*

There must be at least another page, thought Jo. Was 'dear Ann' the Miss Hood whose ideas were so admired by his schoolmistress Mrs. Smith? Who had sent the letter? And what *was* the Recent Discovery?

Well, Mrs. Corbett was sure to know. He folded the letter carefully along its existing crease lines and stowed it deep in his trouser pocket. After his home chores, after his shop chores, after his school hours, he would call on Mrs. Corbett. He would show her the letter.

Then the baby stirred, and emitted its first tiny wail of the day. The other children began to climb from slumber to wakefulness. William sat up, rubbed his itchy, tousled hair, and blinked. Little Jo could see him struggling to recall what he had to do that day. "Withy cutting, William," he offered. "Mr. Holland. He's paying you to cut from the willows on his Witherley river bank." The older boy yawned, while giving Jo a lazy shove.

"Who wants Holland's stupid baskets? I don't."

"Tell that to Pa!" returned Jo, and disappeared nimbly down the stairs.

Meanwhile, towards the station end of town Mary Corbett smiled into her mirror at her maidservant (also a Mary), who was, with difficulty, pinning a lace cap to Mrs. Corbett's age-thinned hair.

"Well, Mary Simmonds, you've a hard task to make these old bones presentable," owned the mistress. "Now put a little more coal on the fire, then help your shaky mistress to her best place beside the window. Let's see who's about, this sparkling April day."

Gathering her voluminous skirt, in fashion despite her seventy-eight years, she allowed herself to be guided by the elbow to sink into her favourite viewpoint.

"And I'll take a cup of tea. Put the stool beside me."

"Ready for Little Jo," she added.

She adjusted the heavy curtain to maximise her view of the street outside. She took great pleasure - and not a little pride - in her situation as well-placed observer. It was not always so, she thought. I've had my turn of striving. And, comfortable in her plush chair, she fell into the customary retreat of the old: reliving events long gone.

From the dark swathes of a lengthy past, certain scenes would light up for her, like bright cameos.

She imagined she was back in the house she and Joseph bought twenty-eight years ago, the house that was once Theodosia's. She imagined herself where she could see that across the road and uphill to her left the morning bustle of travellers and market traders passed in and out of the Old Swan Inn. A carriage swung round to its yard and was swallowed up. Not as many of those nowadays, she noted, returning to her present, now the railway's come. Why, steam's even ousted the canal trade.

She went back to dreaming that she was in Theodosia's old house. In imagination she looked out opposite and downhill to the right. The most prominent house then was that of Dudley Baxter junior. She smiled. Nothing 'junior' about the Lieutenant Colonel, ever! When old Dudley Baxter died in 1811 his son was much occupied with regimental affairs. The Lieutenant Colonel's lady was glad to have the company of her husband's sister, Mrs. Oliver, during those war years. They had been most fond of books, Mary seemed to recall. They were fortunate that the Reverend Oliver shared and fed their interests.

Theodosia! Mary chuckled quietly to herself. Proximity to the older Baxters was a main attraction for Theodosia when she lived in this house of mine, of course it was. Dear, dear, dear. How she wavered, desiring both position and love, unable to unite the two. Let me see, pondered Mary. I'd been married to my Joe for but one year, living in Blue Bell Yard, when her poor, broken husband died. We tried, Joe and I, we tried always to keep her trysts from him. In her mind's eye Mary replayed the flash of a red velvet skirt whisking through the Blue Bell yard entry, back onto Long Street. She saw Daniel Swann, her neighbour then, sullenly unable to meet her eye. She heard Theodosia trilling her wedding plans, with Thomas hardly cold in the ground.

Ha, but my Joseph had the better of Daniel. He took him into our house, sat him down and made him hear him out.
"Thomas Hear, an honest friend, charged me, Joseph Corbett, with the execution of his will, through which he desires that not one farthing of his wife Theodosia's wealth come into your hands."

How the colour drained from the bonny beau's face! Yet I believe he thought there'd be a way around things. So for years by turns he wheedled or stormed. But in the end Theodosia resolved his dilemma. She ushered him out of her house – my house (her inward gaze recalled her well-appointed sitting room) – and Daniel Swann was mired once again in Blue Bell Yard.

My Joe - loyal friend! I think for him his successful protection of Theodosia's interests made our acquisition of that house all the sweeter.

But, nodded Mary, it was sweet enough without extra sugar. Sweet culmination of years of honest toil (that was Joseph) and a wisely deployed flair for investment (that was Mary).

Her train of thought was broken by shouts of a gang of stonebreakers outside her window, followed by the roar of their stones shunting off their wagon. Good, thought Mary. There'll be a little less mud on my carpet. They're taking advantage of the dry weather to scrape the ruts smooth before topping the road with a new layer of rubble. That's my Thomas's doing. He'll have sorted out this work for those poor souls who can find no other employment.

As Poor Law Guardian her son was not one of those who, holding the same position, despised the indigent. "If a man's willing to work, even if it's only at 6d a day, what pain for him to find none," he would say. That was his way: practical, down-to-earth. He understood the intentions of Joseph Wilday, wished him well, but never would join him in his twice-weekly Bible-reading sessions at the workhouse.
"Why, mother," he'd say, "there's nought but blankness on the face of that poor imbecile they call Poor Tom, were he to hear a thousand parables. Rather give him a blanket and a bowl of broth, say I, and pray for him in your heart"

She dwelt for a while on Poor Tom's little shed tucked beside the gates of the new workhouse up the hill. How the times do change, she noted, thinking how the Hinton's great house once sat on that site.

With the unaccountability of memory, she had a vivid recollection of a chance meeting on that spot beside the marl pool long ago.

It was 1799, for my Elizabeth was but a babe, and I fell a-talking to a fine young man, a stranger, with good cloak and boots, and a Londoner's voice. Like strangers do, when they have a full heart, he told me much. (Though not why he was there that day. Perhaps it was to wind up old business?)

He was Edmund Fleetwood Hinton Cooper - she found that a splendid name – and a carpenter, like her own Joseph. But what lingered most in her memory was his pride in his mother's shrewd and strong dealings, which had pulled him back from threatened poverty, and given him a future. He had conjured a picture of the solemn surroundings of the wood-panelled chambers of Lincoln's Inn, and his annual visits there to collect the income, from Atherstone property, that his mother had ensured for him.

Poverty stalks us all, she thought. Take the Simonds. When Mary Simmonds was a girl, Elizabeth and Edmund had run a promising little family hatting business, quite opposite the Baxters (Not much desired by the Baxters, it had to be said, particularly when the Simonds installed their horse-powered carding machine.) For several years they pursued their trade and business, a whole family heart and soul seeking and endeavouring to get a living as other hat manufacturers were managing to do. But bankruptcy was their end, though Mary never knew the particulars.

But the Simonds's business was so small-scale, she recalled, contrasting it with Weaver and Walsh's mill by the canal bridge. They took it over from Pinchbeck - poor fellow, he never got over that change in his life - and they extended it significantly. Like Joseph Wilday's place, she noted. Industry goes on in 'factories' these days, she mused; the word virtually unknown to her in her youth, certainly not then a word in everyday use, as now.

As if in tune with her train of thought, shouts and young laughter drew her gaze towards the dark bulk of Mr. Wilday's factory. A gaggle of children were leaving, having delivered their daily mid-day provision for one or other of their parents. For sure, conditions were better since Mr. Joseph built his model factory. (Despite workers continuing to utilise buckets of their own urine as an invaluable part of the dying process....a practice which invariably made Mary wrinkle her nose, though she conceded nothing better was known.) And yes indeed, there had been some hard times .....Mary had seen the plight of those workers who, in the damp and cold of February 1834 had walked out in a stand for better conditions, and found the tables turned when Mr. Wilday refused to have them back. A 'Tomfools' Union' he had called it.

Yes, poverty stalks us all. May Little Jo evade it! For if ever a boy deserves success, it's Joseph Asher, brightest star in Mrs. Sophia Smith's Coleshill Street school......

Free now from pressures of time and work, Mary continued her recollections in this way as the day sped by, ministered to with affection by her respected maid, her thoughts at times disturbed, fleetingly, by the shrill whistle of a train approaching the station. The little mantelpiece clock sometimes chimed the hours correctly. She greeted the more frequent errors with amusement. "Young William Hood! His clock repairs as incompetent as his business affairs!"

Elsewhere in the town Little Jo's day proceeded at a far swifter pace, but eventually, his obligations met, it was time to go slake his curiosity. He checked his pocket. The letter was safe.

Rounding the corner of Coleshill Street, intent on his mission, he found his head almost enveloped in the leather apron of Ann Briggs of the Red Lion.
"Have a care, boy," rasped the large landlady. Her elderly frame filled the paving beside the inn's arch, but the cuff she delivered was affectionate.

The collision made Jo take more care. He bent low past the Blue Bell, to avoid any possible calls on his time. All clear! Quickly past Mr. Pinchbeck's yard, then a glance down Druids Arms yard, where a sheet hung across its breadth to air, despite the beer-filled fumes emanating from the inn doorway. No-one at home at Mr. Holland's: still withy cutting, no doubt. There he halted. He need not go as far along the street as Mr. Wilday's hatting works.

Despite the lateness of the afternoon, the factory hissed and clanked and clattered, undimmed even where one or two houses came between it and Long Street. Little Jo was glad no factory crowded *his* yard. He pitied the folk in Binghams Row, directly against the feltmakers' shop at the rear of Wilday's. (A boy at school lived there; most mischievously he would make fun of 'woeful Wilday', mimicking to great comic effect Mr. Wilday's strict requirement for each factory day to begin with prayer, until the schoolfellows were all spluttering with laughter and hiding it from Mrs. Smith.)

Now, there it was, Mrs. Corbett's tall house, beside the White Bear. Keen anticipation took him skipping across the road.

That was unlike the first time he had called there. Then, it was a very small boy burdened with a very large book who dithered on the step, unable to reach the doorknocker, rehearsing his message in his head. "If you please, ma'am, I'm sent here as a shining star by Mrs. Smith to bid you good morning and display to you my reading. If you please, ma'am, I'm to tell you Mrs. Smith believes it is - " (deep breath) " extra-ord-in-ary." Four years on, Jo squirmed to recall the speech.

Mrs. Corbett certainly did find it extraordinary.

The book he lugged with such difficulty was Thomas Malthus's "Essay on the Principle of Population". Little Jo had not understood what he read: *It is an obvious truth.... that population must always be kept down to the level of the means of subsistence....The Author hopes it will appear that in the discussion of this interesting subject he is actuated solely by a love of truth and not by any prejudices against any particular set of men or opinions. The view the Author will give of human life has a melancholy hue but he feels conscious that he has drawn these dark tints from a conviction that they really are in the picture and not from a jaundiced eye or an inherent spleen of disposition.*

Though the full meaning passed him by, (and its relevance to the town), Jo savoured certain phrases then, and still did. *Actuated solely by a love of truth* ran through his head as he wrestled with his arithmetic. *Human life has a melancholy hue* echoed when he helped Mr. Corbett take things to the workhouse.

Jo couldn't remember exactly what Mrs. Corbett said when he finished, (though she asked for the book to be left behind for her further attention). But he remembered one thing, because it had taken him by surprise. "What treasures do you hide in your hidey-hole under the little window that looks out onto the pump?"

"*You* know about *my* hidey-hole? How?"

The old lady had a surprisingly girlish laugh.
"Because I've sung other little children to sleep right there. And they all hid things in the hidey-hole"

And she had gone on to tell him such stories.

She told him she went to live in Blue Bell yard when she married Joseph Corbett. They lived at one end of Joseph's joinery.
"We were Mary and Joseph," she said, "but *our* baby's cradle was sawdust and shavings."
She told him how different people came and lived in the yard for a while, then moved on. Often they moved on to live somewhere better, like Joseph's apprentice John Taylor – they had been sad when he left, but saw he must make his own way.

Sometimes people struggled to make a living. "In your father's shop there was Thomas Mottram. Oh my, he thought he could do everything...he was woolcomber, grocer, dealer, pedlar. Borrowed a big sum of money to buy what later became the Blue Bell. I steadied my Joseph when he wanted to do the same. Wait and save, I said. Sure enough, not long after, Mottram had to sell his new purchase – sold it to a butcher, Hickling; his wife it was who opened it as the Blue Bell. And Mottram still borrowed. And borrowed. Asked my help to borrow from *my* family. Even though I got nothing from that quarter myself, but that's another story....."

Mrs. Corbett's frequent half-suggested stories were one reason Jo found his visits so intriguing

"But it didn't work. In the end Mottram went bankrupt." This was the first time Little Jo had heard the word 'bankrupt'. For a while he believed Mottram had turned into a madman.

"Were Mottram's children the children you sang to sleep?"

"Bless you, no. I was too busy singing my own to sleep. No, that was later. But first a saddler, William Webster, he took Mottram's place, stayed for a couple of years, prospered, sold out. But when he sold, he split it in two."

Oh, thought Joseph, that explains the odd shape of our house.

"So," Mrs. Corbett was warming to her tale, "there was William Hood a watchmaker in the front bit, and the Hardings - Messieurs Harding they liked to be called - in the back. And a bit too near us. They were saddlers, like Webster, but they were cow leeches as well."

"Mr. Harding is a cow's leech in our yard now!"

"Exactly. And I'll tell you, Little Jo, I don't think a cow's leech is a good thing in a yard. Listen. The watchmaker's children fell ill, with the terrible fever we call typhus. Summer, it was, and hot. It's stifling in your little bedspace when it's hot, isn't it, Jo? There they lay. Sarah - she was your age, Jo - and Ann, she was eight. The boys were there, too, young William named after his father, and little John - he was never strong. Their lips were caked, faces pale as death, their foreheads all damp, hair clinging to their cheeks. It was hard to heave the water up your stairs, dear Jo, to moisten their dry mouths. Sarah fell into a delirium, calling out that Napoleon was a-coming.... such fanciful things. Then their mother took ill, too. The minister from the chapel in Harris's Coach and Horses yard, he came and prayed, all through one night. Mr. Hood was almost out of his mind. We had Sophia to help, thank God."

The name should have jolted Joseph, but he was too young then to connect it with his schoolmistress.

"And all this while the Hardings kept a sick calf tethered by the pump. Even when I got a chance to sleep, its lowing forbade it. Aye me, Sarah almost slipped away from us then. But we lost little John; for sure he never could have fought it. And their mother died." Mrs.

Corbett paused, in her own thoughts. "So when the children began to recover, it was then that I sang them to sleep. Sophia and me, we sang them to sleep." She paused again. "The following year it was cholera. Sarah went from us that year. She never got over the typhus. It took her strength....." Her voice trailed away.

Recovering her composure, she began to shoo him out. But not without first kissing his forehead – she smelled of lavender – and making him promise to visit again.

Little Jo's second visit was at dusk, the smoky air thickened by the day's sulphurous outpourings of industry. With a seamstress mother dividing her attention between shirts and babies, it wasn't difficult for a boy to slip away. He crossed the stony street, treading carefully between its reminders of thronging, horse-driven traffic. A steam engine was still snorting in a Long Street dye house as he ran past. The tammy weaver Amos Broadby, his day's output of rough webbing on his back, called: "Hey, Jo, where so fast?" but Jo ignored his lurching bonhomie. Charlotte Scott, who'd been a housekeeper at Hams Hall and now ran the King's Arms, mockingly held wide her arms to scoop him up, an embrace he swiftly ducked. He had questions to ask of Mrs. Corbett, and he must be home again before the dangerous hours of dark.

In the wan gaslight of her parlour Mrs. Corbett drew warmth from the boy's energy.

"When did we leave Blue Bell yard? Oh, not for years. I wanted my Joseph to be secure, not speculative...." The story was halted while she explained the word. Little Jo nodded.

"And I learned to be content. When we first went there, we had one of the houses that backs right up against another. Not *completely* against, as you know; there's that narrow space between, all boggy because the rain has nowhere to go. Our bedroom window gave onto this twitchell, but we never opened it –a stagnant swamp below, faughh! I longed to be back near Ratcliffe, among the may flower and the hayfields. But then we moved further down the yard, and my

Joseph in his casting shop made me a little wire fence to mark off a patch of garden ground. Tiny, but it soothed my heart.

"We got on with life. And Jo, there was much life. Sophia Perkins, for one, she brought much life to me in my yard. We took Sophia on once Joseph could afford for me to have help; we took her on for part of the day, as nursemaid."

Little Jo had still not connected Sophia with his school.

"You see, Jo, the rest of the day Sophia was a dressmaker. Not a seamstress making ready-made shirts and so on."
He mentally slotted his mother into this latter category.

"No, she was a dressmaker. She worked for the Quality, making dresses to their exact specification. Mrs. Baxter was her chief patron. And here, Jo, here was a marvellous thing. Mrs. Baxter allowed Sophia to her bookcase. She borrowed books! And brought them to share with me, late in the evenings. 'Have a care for the candles you're consuming,' would grumble my Joseph, yet he loved me to read to him."

"What happened to Mr. Hood the watchmaker and his two children with no mama?"

"Ah, I see you have a memory. Well, Jo, space is the thing, is it not? Room to live? And in the years when his family was increasing, William Hood extended his space by buying the Blue Bell, but he extended his debts along with it, and so was sorely troubled for the rest of his life. He died indebted. Debts are lively things, Jo. One debt can force another. Or your creditor can pass your debt to another, either because he dies, or his circumstances change. I say 'he' and 'his', because it's usually a man. Unless it's an exceptionally astute woman." And here Mrs. Corbett, nodding, placed her hand meaningfully upon her own heart. "So, Little Jo, work to leave the yard, but avoid the clutches of debt."

Jo considered carefully. "Mr. Hood's children, when he died, did they....?"

"Oh my dear, two were grown able to fend for themselves. Young William carried on his father's watch making business. You know John Pinchbeck? He's clever with clocks; the skill runs in the family. He tried to help him. And Ann had her resources. But the third was but a babe."

"The third?"

"Didn't I tell you? Mr. Hood and my comely, clever helpmeet, they married. Sophia Perkins became Mrs. Hood, and brought another little Sophia into the world, step-sister to William and Ann."

Sophia Hood, Sophia Smith....what a lot of Sophias there are, thought Jo.

"Now look how dark it's become! Off you go, young man, and tell your mother it was Mrs. Corbett kept you with her ramblings. And make sure you come again!"

Which Jo did, again and again and again. The old lady and the little scholar loved their shared times, and each other.

So this time now, bearing his letter, it was easy for him to plunge straight in.

"Mrs. Corbett, look: 'My dear Ann'. I think I know...."

At the sight of the letter Mary almost ceased to hear her young visitor's excited commentary. Scenes from earlier times asserted themselves in her mind's eye.

Six children, faces scrubbed, sit in a row on stools and upturned pails by the Blue Bell's back door.

Each holds what seems at first glance to be a hand mirror, but which is actually a hornbook. In unison they chant the alphabet engraved upon the 'books'.

Then, at the bidding of a serious-faced young woman standing before them, they chant the syllables below the alphabet. "ab, eb, ib, ob..." Their childish voices echo between the yard walls. Sophia Hood sits to one side, rocking a wooden cradle with her foot, stitching something black. I was right to supply Ann with hornbooks, thought Mary. That was good use of some of my Joseph's legacy, and it eased the grief of his death. In her memory she hears the children chanting next 'Our Father which art in heaven....'

Two years on, and there is no cradle; diphtheria has snatched the child. Ten children now, they jump up and stack away their stools. There are no more upturned pails. Sophia stands by the passage to Long Street, gravely inclining her head as each child departs. Ann Hood, her step-daughter, stands with a fresh-faced young man, a good ten years her senior. She teases him with a confidence based on equal ambition. "So the time is soon, is it, Mr. Seth Clarke, master grazier, that you take your agricultural skills to the New World? How will Sharnford fare without you?"

Seth responds with kindly respect.
"I have no further life-saving acts to perform here, Miss Ann. You know my pride at having helped your father with some small fraction of the Clarke family moneys. Now thanks to Sophia his property mantle falls on you. Be assured my wife and I believe you will flourish. We urge you: hold firm to your aim to bring the Blue Bell back to the Hoods."
Neither feels the need to mention her brother's struggling business efforts.
"With revenue from the inn, and other rents, dear lady, you can freely pursue a path in education. Continue, do, in your own search for new and better ways to light children into reading"

Then Mary's memory leapt ten years, presenting her with another vignette.

It is the end of a warm May day. She walks with Sophia and Ann, taking the evening air, strolling through the Brickles where the brick kilns used to be, out over the bridge towards the Outwoods. Sophia holds an early hedge rose plucked for her by Mr. John Smith, who accompanies them.

Their discussion is of Martin's New Intellectual Primer, lent to them by Mr. Charles Bray of Coventry, ribbon-weaver by trade and educator by inclination. They note that although Martin disapproves of 'the absurd notion that reading may be taught without Learning to Spell', he nevertheless lists eighteen words to be learned by sight.

Ann glows with eagerness. "There is a truth in this. Let us apply it to the pupils in our care."

She needs no consent from Mary. Mary may have helped her set up school with Sophia in Coleshill Street, (she even put up the money for Ann's successful bid at the auction in the Three Tuns, when she recovered the Blue Bell), but the fizz of ideas is always all Ann's own. Nor does Ann need consent from Mr. Smith. Although he bid at auction on her behalf, and will marry her stepmother Sophia, he recognises scholarly innovation as Ann's domain.

Then Mary - the Mary who had almost lived her life - felt a tug at her sleeve. Outside the western sun sloped low along the length of Long Street. Little Jo was reaching the end of his explanation.

".......so that's why I think, Mrs. Corbett, that Sophia is my Sophia Smith my teacher, and I think 'my dear Ann' is the lady called Miss Hood, who Mrs. Smith sometimes mentions when she gives the little ones their primer "The Anti-Spelling Book". And it makes Mrs. Smith sad, but only for a moment, then she cheers up and says what good things Miss Hood did and we must be thankful to her even though she's dead now.

"But.... Mrs. Corbett, what *was* the Recent Discovery?"

"Ah ha! For that we need another paper."

It was the work of a moment for Mary to ring for her maid Mary Simmonds, make her request, and be delivered, on a little tray, a faded, yellowing newspaper: The Pennsylvania Prospect, July 1838. It was open at the required page. "Read it for me, Jo. Read from there," said Mary, pointing.

A New Exposition of the Business of Reading
The respected physician John Miller Keagy reports that the whole word method he practises with eminent and acknowledged success reached his attention via a young schoolteacher. This man was talking to a little girl of five who was watching her father milk a cow in his yard near Great Bend. He observed amongst the text of the book in his own hand, the word 'cow'. Pointing to the real cow and the word 'cow' on the page, he made the girl aware of the link between the object and the word. She excitedly took up the book, ran to her mother and said, 'I know what it means. It is a cow just like what papa is milking,' and she pointed out the word to her mother. Thus the reading method Look and Say was born.

Little Jo looked at Mary with round eyes. "And the farmer was......"

"The farmer was Seth Clarke"

For a while child and old woman sat in silence, relishing together a dual sense of Atherstone linked to the big, wide world, and Atherstone their close and complex, compact home.

Finally Jo stood. "I have to go. I think I am needed elsewhere."

She smiled at her young protégé. She had given him a platform on which he would build well.

"Go, my child. I hope to see you many times more."

NOTES TO CHAPTER 7

For this chapter Nat Alcock provided a great deal of information on life in Atherstone's yards generally, and on the Blue Bell Yard in particular.

Judy Vero's history of the Atherstone hatting industry, *A Concern in Trade* (Warwickshire Books, 1995), has proved a useful source. Judy has also provided much incidental information. Val Pickard and Mike Trye have added interesting confirmatory details.

And once again the Manor Court Rolls (see Introduction page 12) are major sources. As before, they supply the names, occupations, circumstances and residences of the Atherstone townsfolk whose lives connect with Little Jo's. And if, as mentioned in the Notes to Chapter 6, the 18th century Court Rolls offered such a wealth of detail that selection of any one story proved hard, that was as nothing compared to the richness of the 19th century records!

Information has also been taken from the Census returns of 1841 and 1851. The 1841 Census, for instance, tells of Sophia Hood, aged between 45-49, a schoolmistress living in Coleshill Street with Ann Hood aged 30, of independent means. The 1851 Census catalogues Joseph Asher, master draper, with a family of eight including his three sons, William 13, Joseph 10, and Thomas 8. (Incidentally, Little Jo is not 'Joe', but 'Jo', as a diminutive of the name he shares with his father).

The website www.bbc.co.uk/history/victorian_britain suggested various details.

The mining references are based on John Austin's notes in (Atherstone) Grapevine No. 38, and further draft notes generously supplied.

John Austin and Judy Vero both tell of the use of urine in the town's manufactories; John, as here in the chapter, describing its use in tanning, Judy noting its use in the hat factories – where the workers themselves provided the necessary.

Much of the detail of the history of the teaching of reading is taken from *Studies in the History of Reading* edited by Greg Brooks and Tony Pugh (United Kingdom Reading Association, 1984). This is the source of the Pennsylvanian anecdote.

Mary Corbett seems to have been a woman of initiative, with interesting intellectual connections. Indentures of assets from Mary to her son Thomas Corbett in January 1850 show Mary as having made a loan to a consortium that included Charles Bray. Charles is described as a Coventry ribbon manufacturer.

Charles Bray is known to have been one of the circle of educated thinkers with whom George Eliot spent time before her move to London. In 1849 Charles Bray and his wife took Mary Ann Evans (George Eliot) on a European holiday after the death of her father. His imagined interest in an Atherstone dame school is in keeping with what is known about him.

In this chapter's heading I have not named the Jamieson brothers, night soil men, as fictional characters. Nevertheless, you will search Atherstone records in vain for any reference to them. Atherstone certainly had such people, but, with faction-writer's licence, I have imported the details of these two particular toilers from Huddersfield, where, according to oral accounts still circulating amongst the elderly when I was a child there in the 1940s, there were indeed two nineteenth century brothers matching that name, trade and description.

The site of the Blue Bell Yard is on the opposite side of Long Street from the market place, midway between Market Street and Church Street, where Master's the bakery is now, nos. 87-89 Long Street. It is on the site of C22 on the 1786 map (see Introduction, page 12).

Theodosia's former house, bought by the Corbetts in 1822, stood in the gap to the north-west of the Black Horse, at approximately today's 152-154 Long Street. It was C72 on the 1786 map.

By the time Little Jo is visiting Mary Corbett she has moved to a house somewhere on the site of today's Library.

The workhouse was on the site of Hester Warwick's "great house" (Chapter 5), and the Hinton's/Hewitt's house (Chapter 6), being approximately the site of today's Regal Court.

Harris's Coach and Horses yard, and the chapel there, (C36 on the 1786 map) were where the Woolpack Way Car Park is today, close to Garner Canning, solicitors.

A chronology for the characters in this story
(fictional and/or conjectured dates asterisked)

1772	Mary Payne born.
1787*	Sophia Perkins born.
1793	Mary Payne has a daughter (also Mary) in the autumn
1793	Mary Payne marries Joseph Corbett. (Joseph appears in Chapter 6 as the friend of Thomas Hear.) They live and work in the yard that would be called the Blue Bell Yard after the public house of that name opens in 1798.
1796	Thomas Corbett born to Mary and Joseph.
1798	Blue Bell public house opens.
1807	William Hood, a watchmaker from Leicester, buys the property across the yard-entry from the Blue Bell. He is married to Mary (nee Frone), and their youngest child is Ann.
1813-1820	Two of the Hood children die, as does their mother.
1813-1820	Daniel Swann living in the Yard.
1822	The Corbetts move into Theodosia's former house
1822	William Hood marries Sophia Perkins. They have a daughter, Sophia, who dies an infant.

June 1826	Seth Clarke (along with Joshua Frone, William's brother-in-law) helps William Hood financially.
1826	Joseph Corbett dies.
1828	William Hood dies.
1828 -1837	Seth Clarke settles in Susquehanna.
1834*	Sophia Hood opens a small dame school in the Yard, with her step-daughter Ann.
1838	Ann Hood buys the Blue Bell
1839*	Sophia and Ann move from the Yard and open a dame school in Coleshill Street.
1841	Ann dies.
	Sometime between the 1841 Census and 1850, Sophia marries John Smith.
1845*	Little Jo begins to attend Sophia's school
May 1850	Mary Corbett dies of pneumonia, aged seventy-eight. Mary Simmonds is present at her death.
October 1850	Sophia Smith dies.

POPULATION GRAPH

The graph shows the estimated growth in the population based on figures from:

The Domesday Survey

The Lay Subsidy Lists mid 14th century

The Hearth Tax Returns mid 16th century

The 1851 Census

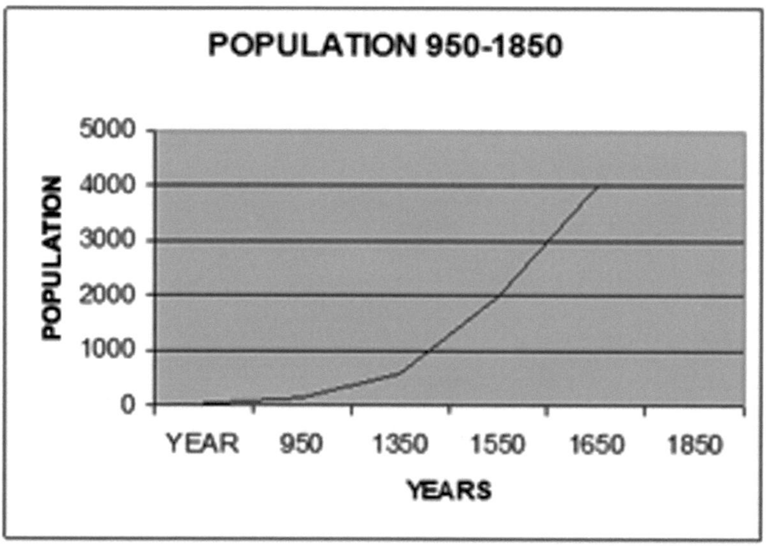